www.wadsworth.com

www.wadsworth.com is the World Wide Web site for Thomson Wadsworth and is your direct source to dozens of online resources.

At *www.wadsworth.com* you can find out about supplements, demonstration software, and student resources. You can also send e-mail to many of our authors and preview new publications and exciting new technologies.

www.wadsworth.com
Changing the way the world learns®

About the Author

Dr. Jane Gaultney is associate professor of Psychology at UNC Charlotte. She has taught Research Methods for many years; never mind *how* many. She received a PhD in Psychology from Florida Atlantic University. Her doctoral training was in cognitive development, and her current research specialization is sleep, cognition and behavior in children.

Doing Research

A Lab Manual for Psychology

Jane F. Gaultney
University of North Carolina at Charlotte

THOMSON

WADSWORTH

Australia • Brazil • Canada • Mexico • Singapore • Spain
United Kingdom • United States

THOMSON
WADSWORTH

Doing Research: A Lab Manual for Psychology
Jane F. Gaultney

Publisher: Vicki Knight

Editorial Assistant: Juliet Case

Technology Project Manager: Erik Fortier

Senior Marketing Manager: Dory Schaeffer

Senior Marketing Communications Manager:
Kelley McAllister

Signing Representative: Tracy Landrum

Project Manager, Editorial Production: Karol Jurado

Creative Director: Rob Hugel

Senior Art Director: Vernon Boes

Print Buyer: Rebecca Cross

Permissions Editor: Kiely Sisk

Production Service: International Typesetting
and Composition

Text Designer: Anne Draus, Scratchgravel

Copy Editor: Prachi Gildiyal

Illustrator: International Typesetting and Composition

Cover Designer: Laurie Albrecht

Cover Image: GeoStock/Getty Images

Cover Printer: Webcom Limited

Compositor: International Typesetting and
Composition

Printer: Webcom Limited

Printed in Canada

1 2 3 4 5 6 7 10 09 08 07 06

Library of Congress Control Number: 2005937323

ISBN 0-495-00571-1

Thomson Higher Education
10 Davis Drive
Belmont, CA 94002-3098
USA

For more information about our products,
contact us at:
Thomson Learning Academic Resource Center
1-800-423-0563

For permission to use material from this text or
product, submit a request online at
http://www.thomsonrights.com.
Any additional questions about permissions can
be submitted by e-mail to
thomsonrights@thomson.com.

To all the students who have survived my class in Research Methods: see, you really could pass the class, and even excel! I hope you're proud of how much you learned and accomplished. I'm proud of you.

To Paul Foos, who said, "You have already written a lab manual; it can't be much more work to publish it." Yes, it can. Thanks for the encouragement.

To Vicki Knight of Thomson/Wadsworth Publishing, who very patiently guided me through the publication process.

Table of Contents

Note to Students

Dear Student,

This Research Methods Lab Manual contains exercises that reinforce concepts presented in most Research Methods textbooks. One can learn *about* research methodology from the textbook, but the only way to learn to *do* research is . . . to do it. These exercises are intended to supplement your textbook and to cement concepts presented in class rather than teach new material. I want to help you add "knowing how" to "knowing about." Do you remember when you first learned to drive? You read the drivers' manual, you learned about how a car operates, you memorized the road signs and driving laws, but learning to get in a car and drive it smoothly required getting in a car and practicing. Knowing *about* driving was important, but wasn't the same thing as knowing *how* to drive.

A secondary purpose is to broaden your concepts of the field of psychology, particularly the breadth of psychological research. For many students, clinical psychology is the only "real" psychology. You've probably already taken an introductory class in Psychology, so you know that Psychology is more than just counseling, but you might not be clear on what sorts of things are studied by the different specialties within Psychology. Each lab will feature an article illustrating a different area of psychology (e.g., social, neurocognitive, health, developmental, etc.) along with a brief description written, in many cases, by someone who specializes in that area. References for all the articles featured in these labs can be found on the student Web site that accompanies this lab manual. In addition, URLs for the Web site featured in the lab manual are provided on the student Web site as "live" links.

I realize many of you have not looked forward to taking Research Methods with a lot of joy. Some of you have been avoiding it for years! I hope that by the end of this class you will appreciate the value of your new knowledge about research. Even if you do not pursue a career in research, there will be times when you are asked to assemble, interpret, and communicate data, and the skills you acquire in Research Methods can help you do that. Just the other day I saw an employment ad for someone with a bachelor's degree with experience in collecting and analyzing data. Furthermore, you are, and always will be, a consumer of research, and the more you know about research the better you can evaluate what you are told (e.g., "9 out of 10 doctors agree . . ."). Finally, I hope that you will discover the *fun* of doing research. Research is somewhat like a treasure hunt—you never know what you're going to find!

Dr. Jane Gaultney
Psychology
UNC Charlotte

Note to Instructors

This lab manual has grown out of activities that I have developed over many years of teaching Research Methods. It is intended to supplement—not replace—traditional textbooks in research methodology. It probably is most useful for those departments that offer research methods with an accompanying lab. My goal is to help students make the leap from learning about research to learning how to carry it out. We don't expect most undergraduate students to produce publishable research at the end of this class—if we can just get them to be a little excited about the possibilities of doing research, then we've accomplished a lot. Although some of my colleagues find it a bit strange, Research Methods is my favorite class to teach. Not only do I love research, but this course allows me to do more hands-on teaching than is possible in a large lecture course, and students make so much progress throughout the class. OK, *most* of them make a lot of progress!

The labs have been arranged to be consistent with the steps students take to do a term-long research project, all the way from coming up with a topic to producing a finished, APA-style paper. You can, of course, present them in any order that is most useful to your students, and pick and choose the ones most relevant to your curriculum.

Several articles are featured in various labs in this manual. In some labs the articles are used as teaching tools or for exercises. In most cases it is *not* necessary that students have access to that particular article; you can substitute another article that is available to them. The articles are listed, in order of appearance (rather than alphabetically), on the password-protected Web site that accompanies this lab manual in case you wish to look ahead and obtain copies of these articles. Again, students can do most of the assignments in this lab manual using any appropriate article you assign. One option is to have them apply the lessons of various labs to articles they have included in a literature review.

In addition, URLs for the Web sites featured in the lab manual are provided on the instructors' Web site as "live" links.

I would like to thank the following reviewers whose insightful comments and suggestions greatly improved this manual.

Grant Benham
University of Texas-Pan American

James Eubanks
Central Washington University

Tim Goldsmith
University of New Mexico

Elliott Hammer
Xavier University

Marjorie Hardy
Eckerd College

David Jones
Westminster College

Shannon Mihalko
Wake Forest University

Nancy Minahan
University of Wisconsin-Superior

John Murray
Georgia Southern University

Louise Perry
Florida Atlantic University

Jane F. Gaultney

Part I

Preparing to Design a Study

Finding a Topic

The Field of Psychology

When I first thought about majoring in psychology, I assumed my career would involve some aspect of counseling or providing therapy—in other words, clinical psychology. I didn't consider any other area of psychology because that was the only area of psychology I knew about. I soon learned that psychology encompasses many different specialties, each of which explores a different aspect of human behavior or characteristics. Throughout this lab manual you'll read about just a few of the many faces of psychology.

Psychology can initially be subdivided into two approaches: experimental and applied. Experimental psychology works to add to our body of knowledge about human behavior by conducting research projects. Experimental psychology can be broken down into many areas, some of which you'll read about here. All psychological research, regardless of the subject matter, uses research methodology, some of which you'll learn about in this class. Applied psychology applies the knowledge of human behavior to some setting. Two major branches of applied psychology are clinical psychology and industrial/organizational psychology (the application of psychology to business). Of course, some psychologists are involved both in research and application.

Psychologists are employed in a number of different types of jobs. Some are in private practice, some work for agencies, some are employed by businesses, and some work at universities or for the government. Some create new knowledge, while others apply that knowledge to helping people improve their personal lives, productivity, or to inform public policy. According to the American Psychological Association* (APA), 10 percent of psychologists work for nonprofit agencies, 10 percent in government, 34 percent in universities, 6 percent in

* http://www.apa.org/students/brochure/brochurenew.pdf

other educational settings, 18 percent are self-employed, and 22 percent work in a for-profit business.

 As you go through this class keep your mind open about just what psychology entails. You may find a career opportunity that you'd never thought about before. For more information about graduate training and careers in psychology, check out http://www.apa.org/students/.

Assignment

Your instructor may ask you to complete a research assignment during this term. The labs in this manual are designed and organized to help you carry out your project. The first step is to identify a topic that you will study. The purpose of this lab is to help you come up with a short list of potential topics that you'd like to learn more about. You will eventually choose one of these areas for an individual project. Turn in: a list of possible topics for your project.

Where Do I Find a Topic Idea?

The topic for your research project should be something that really interests you. It's going to be a lot of work, so it will be best if you like your topic. Begin by thinking about areas of psychology that have interested you as you studied them in other classes. Skim through different psychology textbooks, looking for a small *subheading* (a major heading probably covers too broad an area for your paper) that looks interesting. Once you have several topic ideas in mind, do some reading about each one. You can read about them in textbooks (perhaps your instructor, your library, or your peers have textbooks from various areas of psychology you can peruse) and in journals. For example, in a chapter on biological bases of behavior you see a section on emotions, and a subheading on cross-cultural similarities/ differences in the expression of emotions. If that interests you, then pursue it.

Use a search engine such as PsycINFO or InfoTrac® College Edition (available through Thomson/Wadsworth) to help you locate journal articles relating to your topic. Search the Internet for Web sites that relate to your topic (remembering that some Web sites are more reliable than others). Use these sources to help you narrow down your topic to a manageable size. For example, I opened PsycINFO and entered "memory" and got over 96,000 entries. I then tried "infants and memory" and whittled it down to just over 1000 entries. I then tried "infants, memory and cocaine" and got 10 entries on the effects of prenatal cocaine exposure on early memory. Now I'm down to a topic that has a manageable size. At this point you aren't reading articles in detail; you are just skimming to get the general idea.

Other Sources . . .

1. Look online. Check the following Web sites: http://www.merlot.org/artifact/ BrowseArtifacts.po?catcode=25&browsecat=19—there are literally hundreds of demonstrations and experiments to look at. You can see those relevant to a specific area of psychology by clicking the arrow in front of "psychology." Another source that is not specific to psychology but may have useful ideas is http://library.uncc.edu/display/?dept=reference &format=standard&page=174. Check out the demonstrations at https:// implicit.harvard.edu/implicit/demo/.

2. Another resource I found recently on the Centers for Disease Control Web site is http://www.cdc.gov/ncipc/pub-res/pdf/sec1.pdf. This is a collection of attitude and belief assessment instruments. Go to http://www. cdc.gov/ncipc/pub-res/pdf/sec2.pdf for a collection of psychological and cognitive assessment instruments related to youth violence. Change the 2 in the URL to a 3 and you find assessments for behaviors related to youth violence. Change it to 4 and you get assessments of parent, family and community influences on youth. Even though all these instruments are intended for children and adolescents, you may be able to adapt them for other populations. Remember that younger college students might still be considered adolescents. You may find a topic that interests you even if you don't want to use one of these instruments.

3. Is there some aspect of human behavior that has always puzzled or intrigued you? What topic caught your attention in your introductory psychology course? This could be your opportunity to answer your questions. What can you find about that aspect of behavior in the literature?

4. Your instructor may have a collection of idea starters—ask what is available.

Keep a list of topics that catch your attention as you search. Narrow down that list to your three favorites, then explore those three in more detail. Your instructor may want you to submit one or more topic ideas for approval.

Reality Check

If your instructor is going to have you collect data on your topic at some point down the road, you may need to keep in mind some of the realities of your situation as you choose your topic. For example, unless you already have access to children (or prisoners, or other protected groups) you may not be able to carry out a study of that population. In other words, don't choose to study prosocial behavior in 4-year-olds unless you have access to a group of 4-year-olds. Ditto for animal research—don't go there if you don't have access to an animal lab.

Not all research topics are created equally. There are some perfectly interesting topics that aren't amenable to scientific study. You may be convinced that watching sunsets is a cure for stress, but there may not be any scholarly research available. If you can't find anything about it in the peer-reviewed journals, then pick something else. If, however, you do decide to collect data on sunset-watching, let me know and I'll volunteer to be a participant!

It's OK to change horses in midstream. You may get started on a topic and decide it is a dead end or just not something you want to spend a lot of time on. In that case, change topics (unless, of course, it is the day before your paper is due) to something more productive.

What are the Steps of a Research Project?

Now that you've identified a topic, what happens next? It might be useful to write in a date when each of these steps should be started and completed. Don't feel overwhelmed by all that has to be done for a research project. Take one step at a time. This lab manual will assist you with some of these steps.

1. Review the literature. Read about your topic in the professional journals and books. This will be the basis for your literature review paper (which becomes the introduction section of your final paper).
2. Develop a research question.
3. Develop a hypothesis based on a relevant theory.
4. Design a study that will adequately test your hypothesis. This includes identifying the design you'll use, who your participants will be, the materials you'll use, the exact procedure you'll follow as you collect your data, and the statistic(s) you'll use to analyze your data.
5. Have your study approved by an Institutional Review Board (IRB). In some cases your instructor may serve as the IRB for a classroom project.
6. Collect data.
7. Analyze and interpret your data.
8. Report your findings. You may do this by means of a poster, orally in a presentation, or in written form (or perhaps all of the above).
9. Use your findings as a springboard for the next project. OK, so maybe you won't have time to do another project for this class, but it is a good exercise to always be thinking ahead to the next project.

Now Do It

Look through the sources indicated above and generate a short list of possible topics. It might be a good idea to indicate where you found each topic so you can go back to it later.

Closure

Consider the advice of Mark Twain. "*The secret of getting ahead is getting started. The secret of getting started is breaking your complex overwhelming tasks into small manageable tasks, and then starting on the first one.*" This lab manual teaches one aspect of your final project at a time. Don't worry about all the assignments you have for this class. Just organize what you need to do into smaller steps, and do one small step at a time.

Obtain a calendar or work planner. Look over all the assignments you have for this course. Write down when each one is due, as well as when each one should be started. For example, enter the date a paper is due, then back up several weeks to decide when you must begin it. Allow yourself time to write several drafts of any written assignment.

Finding and Critically Reading Appropriate Articles

Developmental Psychology

Developmental psychologists examine changes in physical, cognitive, or social functions as they are manifested from conception to older adulthood. Researchers may focus on these changes as they occur in infants, children, adolescents, or adults (usually older adults). Rather than study these topics frozen at one point of development, they study the ways in which these processes and characteristics change as individuals get older. Others study how development is impacted by the circumstances in which one grows up, such as families, schools, and neighborhoods. Some developmental psychologists study age-related changes in other species. Knowledge of developmental psychology helps parents, teachers, and others who work with children better understand the changes children experience as they get older. It helps those who make policies know how best to help children.

Examples of research in this area might include the development of aggression, interactions between family style and type of community and their effects on children's development, changes in memory across childhood or into older adulthood, or changes in the development of spatial perception. Some may study the effects of harmful substances on human or rat fetuses. This is only a small sampling of the types of things studied by developmental psychologists.

 For some humor about childhood and developmental psychology go to http://www.devpsy.org/humor/index.html. The Society for Research in Child Development publishes the journal *Child Development*. See their Web site http://www.srcd.org/. The APA publishes the journal *Developmental Psychology*, http://www.apa.org/journals/dev.html. See a description of developmental psychology at The Psi Café, http://www.psy.pdx.edu/PsiCafe/Areas/Developmental/.

Assignment

For this lab you will find and analyze an article having to do with one of the topics you chose in the last lab. Turn in: completed "Review of Article Form" found at the end of this lab.

Topic

Gender differences in mate preferences of teenagers

Target Article

> Kenrick, D. T., Keefe, R. C., Gabrielidis, C., & Cornelius, J. S. (1996). Adolescents' age preferences for dating partners: Support for an evolutionary model of life-history strategies. *Child Development, 67*(4), 1499–1511.

Which seems to make more sense to you—an older woman dating a younger man, or an older man dating a younger woman? You're likely to choose the latter configuration. Is it just a western cultural thing, or is it a common pattern throughout the world? According to Kenrick et al. (1996), it appears to be common in many cultures. Evolutionary psychology suggests that this aspect of human behavior may have evolved because younger women are likely to be more fertile than older women, and therefore are more attractive to older men. If fertility rather than age is the determining factor, then adolescent males should be attracted to slightly older women, again for their greater fertility relative to teenaged girls. The authors interviewed over 200 adolescents aged 12 to 19, as to their date preferences. As predicted, males indicated that although they'd be willing to date someone slightly below their age, they preferred to date someone older than themselves. Adolescent females, however, indicated they preferred to date someone their own age or slightly older—just like older females.

Tips for Finding Articles

The following information is somewhat generic, and may or may not reflect sources available to you through your library. Information specific to your library will be most useful for you. Find out if your library offers classes on how to find research sources. If such instruction is available to you, take advantage of it.

1. Evaluating Web sites: For assistance in evaluating Web sites see http://library.uncc.edu/webeval/.

2. Locating Articles: Databases and indexes will vary by library, but some general issues are:

A. *Selecting the appropriate database.* There are many databases to choose from but not all of them are appropriate for a particular discipline or topic. There are "interdisciplinary" databases such as "Academic Search Elite" (that include psychology along with literature, education, business, politics, sociology, the sciences, etc.), but also discipline-specific databases such as PsycINFO. While interdisciplinary databases will cover subjects in a specific discipline, the discipline-specific databases offer greater depth and breadth. The examples given here use PsycINFO.

Many times students are tempted to skip the academic search engines, and search "Yahoo" or "Google" for the information they need. Why shouldn't you do this since it is often easier and more familiar? There is a great deal of interesting, helpful stuff on the Internet, but in most cases it hasn't met the scientific standard of peer-review. The peer-review process is a method for ensuring that what gets published has been carefully thought through, properly carried out, and appropriately analyzed and interpreted. It acts as a filter that prevents substandard or incomplete research from being circulated. Web sites and non-peer-reviewed journals could give you anything from high-quality information to useless or inaccurate information.

B. *Selecting appropriate terminology.* Some disciplines (like psychology) have their own vocabulary and so using the correct terms is important. Students need to learn the terminology of their discipline. This is especially important when searching a database like PsycINFO that uses APA-defined terms. If you are not successful searching a particular term, click the "Thesaurus" tab, type in your search term—for example, "self concept"—then click "Go To Terms." Searching on the thesaurus terms provides more relevant entries. However, there may not be a thesaurus or the thesaurus terms may not be exactly what are needed. In that case, consult psychology textbooks or ask instructors for suggested terms.

C. *Developing appropriate search strategies.* Once you have thesaurus terms or key terms you will need to create a strategy that will provide relevant results. This is where the use of boolean (or logical) operators and "nesting" play a part. You can combine terms so the "logic" retrieves entries that are very specific to your topic. For example, if you are interested in the development of self-concept, click on the "Advanced" search tab in PsycINFO, then specify terms, linking them using the search terms, "and," "or," or "not." If you were interested in self-concept in children you could enter "self-concept" as a subject and "children" as a subject, linking them with the word "and." This would limit your results to just those dealing with self-concept and children, as opposed to self-concept at any age.

D. *Selecting appropriate types of materials.* You should use peer-reviewed/scholarly materials in your literature review. These include articles published in a professional journal as well as chapters in books that have undergone a peer-review process. Some databases (like Academic Search Elite) provide an option to limit a search just to the peer-reviewed/scholarly literature. Other databases do not provide any option and students have to "know" the difference. In that case, your instructor can steer you toward appropriate journals. Others, like PsycINFO, include only scholarly articles (a subset of which is peer-reviewed).

E. *Database features.* Each database has options/features that can assist the student in retrieving the desired results. Think about exactly what you want, then see if the database lets you limit your search based on your needs. For example, "Academic Search Elite" includes articles in popular magazines, newspaper articles, and articles in peer-reviewed/scholarly journals. You can set the limit to scholarly, peer-reviewed journals; that way you won't have to wade through long lists of references you can't use. It also allows you to specify the time-period to be searched (e.g., articles published since 1999), what fields (subject, keyword, author, etc.) to be searched, and whether or not to limit the output to just what is available full-text (if the database offers that). This last item is tempting because students often want only full-text. They don't want a citation that they then will have to find in print or will have to order through interlibrary loan. However, if they limit the search just to full-text, they may be missing important articles. Be willing to actually go into the library and find the hard copy of a particular journal.

Another example is PsycINFO. Students can manipulate the database so they retrieve what they want. Decisions to be made here include (1) English-language materials, (2) peer-reviewed journal articles (or publication type—journals, rather than books, chapters, or dissertations), (3) population (human, animal), (4) dates to be searched, (5) empirical research, etc.

Some articles relevant to psychology aren't listed by PsycINFO because they are primarily associated with other disciplines. For example, you might search PubMed if you were studying health psychology. You should search journals specific to criminal justice, communication, business, education, and so on if your topic of interest overlaps with another discipline.

How to Read an Article

OK, so you've found your article. Now what? There is a method for reading an article critically. You are now going to work through an online tutorial that will make this method explicit.

 Go to: http://www.psych.ualberta.ca/~varn/Kenrick/Reading.htm.

In order to complete this assignment you'll need to look at the original article, which was listed above as the target article. You may be able to access an online version of this article or get a hard copy of it through your library.

Kenrick, D. T., Keefe, R. C., Gabrielidis, C., & Cornelius, J. S. (1996). Adolescents' age preferences for dating partners: Support for an evolutionary model of life-history strategies. *Child Development, 67*(4), 1499–1511.

Start with "Questions to Consider" in the tutorial and go through each section of the paper, answering questions as you go (click on the green check marks). First read the section in the original article, then read the online comments about that section and answer the questions.

Put It into Practice

Now it is your turn. Use keywords to search PsycINFO or some other search engine for an article related to your topic. Obtain the entire article, not just the abstract. Read the article, then answer the questions below as they relate to your article. Be sure to read the "Closure" section of this lab before you begin to fill in the Review of Article Form.

Looking Ahead

Go ahead and begin collecting articles that pertain to the topic you've chosen. We'll be using them in a later lab.

Closure

Here are some points to consider as you read about a study. Some of these questions may require more knowledge than you have at this point, and you will not be able to answer them. They are included here just to let you know that they are important considerations.

Introduction

Who wrote the article and in which journal was it published?

What was the research question or hypothesis (some studies will have more than one)?

What background information was cited that led to the formation of this question?

Does the research address an important issue?

Method

Who were the participants, and how were they recruited? Are they appropriate for this particular research question?

What design was used for the study? Is the design appropriate to address the research question?

What measures were used? How were they operationalized?* Do they measure what the author really wants to measure (in other words, are they valid)?

What ethical issues apply to this study? Were they addressed?

Were any extraneous variables identified? How were they controlled?

Results

What were the main findings of the study?

Do these results address the research question?

Were appropriate statistical analyses performed?

Discussion

What conclusions did the author draw from the results? Are the conclusions justified based on the results?

How do these findings relate to the literature (e.g., do they confirm earlier studies? Contradict? Raise new questions?)?

To what extent can the findings be generalized?

---

*"*Operationalized*" refers to defining an abstract construct—like self-esteem or depression—in terms of a behavior that can be observed and measured. For example, anxiety is abstract and can't be directly observed, but since feeling anxious can raise one's heart rate you can operationalize anxiety as a rise in heart rate as compared to a baseline.

Review of Article Form

Author(s)*_____ Year of publication_____

    Title (Use all lower case letters except proper names, 1st word of title, 1st word after colon) _____

    Journal name (Use title case and italicize) _____

    Vol. # (italicize)_____, p. ____–____.

* List authors by last name followed by initials, e.g. Smith, J. L., in the same order in which they appear.

Topic and purpose of the study _____

Hypothesis _____

How investigated _____

_____

_____

_____

_____

Results _____

_____

_____

_____

Interpretation _____

_____

_____

_____

Criticism or alternative explanations _____

_____

_____

_____

Additional research to do _____

_____

_____

_____

Ethics of Research

Social Psychology

DR. JENNIFER WELBOURNE

Social psychology is the scientific study of the way in which people's thoughts, feelings, and behaviors are influenced by others. Social psychologists have a strong interest in how people are influenced by the social situation that they are in. Some examples of the topics that social psychologists conduct research on include: how people form impressions of one another; why people become attracted to one another; what types of situations lead to violent behavior; why people are prejudiced against members of certain groups; and how people influence and persuade one another. While many social psychologists conduct basic research to understand the processes that underlie these phenomena, others conduct applied research to see how these same concepts can be used in legal, health, business, and other types of settings. Social psychologists use a variety of both lab and field studies to examine their research questions. For instance, a social psychologist might study attraction by conducting a laboratory study in which participants view pictures of people and rate how attractive they are or by conducting a field study to watch how people meet and attract at a dance or at a bar.

One of the primary types of research designs used by social psychologists is the experiment. Social psychologists often examine interaction effects, to look at how aspects of both the situation and the person jointly influence the variables that they are measuring. A number of social psychology experiments have become well-known for the ethical questions they have raised. A prime example is Stanley Milgram's study on obedience, where participants were led to believe that they were delivering shocks to an innocent person at the demand of the experimenter. Although no one actually gave or received any shocks in this study (the researchers were merely testing whether participants would be willing to obey orders given by an authority figure), this research study raised many questions about the use of deception in research and whether debriefing could adequately remove emotional stress endured by participants during the research.

Assignment

This lab will consider the ethical treatment of participants and the ethics of reporting research. You will turn in the following:

1. a short (2 pages) paper on plagiarism—sources will be listed below,
2. historical reasons for the formal protection of research participants,
3. a statement (listed below) that you have completed a tutorial on treatment of human subjects and one on treatment of animals,
4. and identification of ethical concerns in several different studies.

Topic

How to treat participants (human or otherwise)

Target Article

Haney, C., & Zimbardo, P. (1998). The past and present of U.S. prison policy. *American Psychologist, 53*(7), 709–727.

A copy of this article can be found at http://www.prisonexp.org/pdf/ap1998.pdf.

This is a review article prompted by a famous social psychology experiment conducted by Philip Zimbardo at Stanford University in the early 1970s. This isn't a research report; it is a review of related research and consideration of its implications for prison policy and reform. Read this article and an overview of the experiment at http://www.prisonexp.org/ and then briefly describe the ethical dilemma that emerged (unexpectedly) during this study, and how the experimenter handled it. Can you think of any recent examples of the social dynamics that became apparent during this experiment?

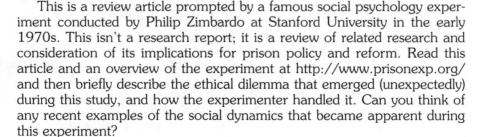

_____

_____

_____

_____

_____

_____

_____

_____

At most institutions you must receive the approval of an Institutional Review Board (IRB) before beginning any experiment that involves collecting data from humans or animals. This has not always been the case. At one time researchers could design and carry out their experiments without any oversight. However, a number of events convinced people that oversight is a good thing. Read the article at http://www.stanford.edu/dept/DoR/hs/History/his01.html and identify several historical events that helped convince scientists that research using human subjects must be regulated. Name at least three (using only one example of Nazi research).

_____

_____

_____

How to Treat Human and Animal Subjects

Go to http://www.research.uncc.edu/tutorial/index3.cfm. Log on as a guest and complete the human subjects tutorial and the animal subjects tutorial. Sign and turn in this page to document your completion of these tutorials.

I have completed the human subjects tutorial. _____
                                                                (signature)

I have completed the animal subjects tutorial. _____
                                                                (signature)

The human subjects tutorial indicates that participants should have the opportunity to give informed consent. Lab 7 contains an example of a form you can use to obtain informed consent.

Given what you've learned from these tutorials, identify ethical issues raised by the studies described in the following five sources. How did the experimenter deal with the ethical issues? Should more have been done to protect the participants? If so, what? Was the information gained worth the risks? Are there examples of studies that simply should not have been conducted because of ethical concerns? You can write your answers on your own paper.

1. http://users.rcn.com/napier.interport/cwm/experim.html (scroll down to the section entitled "Controversial Experiments."
2. http://online.sfsu.edu/~psych200/unit10/104.htm
3. Norman Maier's use of shock to make rats jump in the jumping stand; he thought he had discovered experimental neurosis because the animals developed seizures. Actually, it was the noise that triggered the seizures. Maier's work is described in *American Psychologist*, 1993, 869–877.
4. http://www.npr.org/programs/morning/features/2002/jul/tuskegee/
5. For a "Chronology of Human Research" see http://www.ahrp.org/history/chronology.php

Ethical Reporting of Research: How Do I Know If It Is Plagiarism?

You already know that when you turn in a paper that claims to be original writing it must not contain any plagiarized material. In order to avoid plagiarizing, you have to know exactly what it is. Using the instructions below, write a brief paper on plagiarism. The aim of the paper is to teach the reader what plagiarism is and how to avoid it. You will use at least three sources: the section in your Research Methods textbook (or a similar textbook) on plagiarism, the *APA Publication Manual* (cited below; look up "plagiarism" in the index), and a Web site. Go to http://www.Turnitin.com/research_site/e_home.html and look at the sites listed for students. Cite at least one of these sites. You may use additional sources if you wish to do so. Check the Web site of your institution to see if there is a policy in place regarding plagiarism. How does it define plagiarism? Does it specify the consequences of plagiarism? Be sure to read "Tips for Avoiding Plagiarism" in the Closure section below before you begin to write.

Include a title page, two pages of *original* writing summarizing the three sources (use APA citations in the body of your paper—see p. 207–214, *APA Publication Manual,* 5th ed.), and a reference page.

American Psychological Association. (2001). *Publication Manual of the American Psychological Association* (5th ed.). Washington, D.C.: Author.

See the *APA Publication Manual,* p. 268 ff, or check http://www.apsu.edu/~lesterj/cyber4.htm to find the proper way to cite your electronic source(s).

Other Ethical Issues

Even though we won't go into it in detail, there are other ethical concerns in research. For example, there are ethical and unethical ways to analyze and report your data. If you have promised your participants confidentiality or anonymity, then you have an ethical responsibility to make sure you carry out that promise. If you heard someone talking about his or her research idea (or perhaps reviewed a manuscript for a journal), then you cannot use that idea without crediting the originator. To see what the APA has to say about the ethics of research and publication, see section 8 at http://www.apa.org/ethics/code2002.html.

Closure

Tips for Avoiding Plagiarism

1. Close all sources when you write. You aren't likely to copy something you can't see.
2. Taking notes: make notations in your own words, making sure you have written down complete source information, including the page number. If you wish to put the author's exact words in your notes, make sure you indicate this by using quotation marks.
3. If you do use a direct quote in your paper (you should use these sparingly), you must put it in quotation marks, and indicate the source and the page number. See p. 117–118 in the *APA Publication Manual*.
4. Identify the source of the ideas or findings and summarize in your own words what was said. Using the author's words while changing a few words is still plagiarism. Some sources define plagiarism as any use of four or more contiguous words.
5. Reference the source of anything that is not common knowledge. For example, you don't need to document the source when you state that plagiarism is not acceptable in professional writing; you do need to cite the source if you claim that 40% of student papers submitted in college courses contain plagiarism. By the way, I just made up that last statistic for the sake of providing an example.

Using APA Style Writing

Community Psychology

DR. RYAN KILMER

Several factors led to the development of Community Psychology (CP), including a growing dissatisfaction with mental health's traditional reactive, problem-focused approach. Although psychology often emphasized what went wrong and how to "fix" it, CP's founders recognized that treatment is not the only way to address mental health and psychosocial problems. As such, CP includes an emphasis on working to change (i.e., improve) systems and environments in a way that enhances quality of life for individuals and communities. Thus, the nature and level of operation is distinct from clinical work; rather than intervening with specific individuals, CPs tend to work with systems, communities, neighborhoods, and programs in ways that can benefit people, as well as the larger community. The prevention of mental, emotional, or behavioral problems before they occur, and the promotion of wellness (i.e., positive mental health, healthy adaptation) are other key foci of this relatively young field.

Efforts in CP encompass a diverse range of domains—working with neighborhood organizations to empower citizens and help build on community strengths; establishing curricula to foster the development of social and emotional competencies; developing interventions for children of divorce; addressing the needs of refugee groups and assessing the efficacy of resettlement programs; researching child resilience to better understand factors that may serve a protective function and facilitate positive adjustment despite adversity, so that such knowledge can inform prevention programs for at-risk youngsters.

One of the biggest challenges facing those working within CP is that they are conducting research in the real-life community environment, a setting much different from the laboratory. Such work is fraught with variables and conditions that cannot be controlled. Community researchers often employ matched comparison groups to assess the effectiveness of a program or intervention; however, even with an optimal match, other factors and circumstances can come into play and impact outcomes. Furthermore, CPs often work with vulnerable and diverse populations. In turn, this requires awareness of ethnic and cultural differences and, often, adapting one's research approach out of sensitivity to the culture of those being studied. In general, CPs collaborate with community partners to employ both qualitative (e.g., focus groups, interviewing, participant observation) and quantitative (e.g., randomized field experiments when possible, comparison group designs, use of interrupted time-series designs, collecting data before and after interventions) methods to study phenomena of interest.

For additional information on CP see the following reference:

Dalton, J. H., Elias, M. J., & Wandersman, A. (2001). *Community psychology: Linking individuals and communities.* Stamford, CT: Wadsworth/Thomson Learning.

Assignment

The goal of this lab is to write a literature review using proper APA style. Detailed instructions for writing a literature review are given in Appendix 1. Turn in: a literature review on your topic written in correct APA style.

Topic

Stressful life experiences among three groups of homeless adults

Target Article

Zugazaga, C. (2004). Stressful life event experiences of homeless adults: A comparison of single men, single women, and women with children. *Journal of Community Psychology, 32*(6), 643–654.

This article found that different groups of homeless individuals have had different life histories, and suggests that intervention efforts should be tailored to each group. In other words, with regard to intervention, one size doesn't fit all. The study examined the experiences of single men, single women, and women with children. They found that women were more likely to have experienced physical and sexual abuse during their childhood. Single women were more likely to have experienced sexual abuse as adults (over age 18), to have lived with domestic violence, and to have been hospitalized for psychiatric problems. Single men were more likely to have experienced substance abuse or to have spent time in jail. Women with children were more likely than the other groups to have spent time in foster care. Of the three groups, single women had experienced the most stressful life events.

Learning to Write Using APA Style

Teaching someone to write well goes far beyond the scope of this lab manual. The way to improve your writing is to read well-written papers (lots of them) and to write, get feedback, then rewrite. And rewrite again. My advisor in graduate school once said that if you have done only one draft of a paper, then all you have done is typed. Good writing involves multiple drafts before a final product is ready.

Today we'll learn some of the mechanics of APA style. This is the format used by professionals in psychology and other related disciplines. The page numbers given in this lab refer to the *Publication Manual of the American Psychological Association,* 5th edition. It is quite possible that your textbook also has a chapter on APA style and can be a resource for you to use with this lab.

First of all, writing a literature review may require a different style of writing than you used for your English class. The purpose of the literature review is to summarize the existing literature on some topic; therefore, you are synthesizing factual information from primary sources (articles that reported research). Try to write the review as if you are telling the story of some topic, not just listing a bunch of studies one after the other. Here are some pointers on this type of writing:

1. Scientific writing—especially the literature review portion—is a presentation of the existing material on a particular topic. For example, if your paper is about the effect of depression on memory performance, you would locate a number of research papers on that topic, read them, think about how they contribute toward the "story" of depression and memory, then write about that topic, citing the papers as they support your points. This is not an essay. The literature review is a chance to summarize the existing literature—opinions and anecdotes don't belong here.
2. You have a responsibility in your literature review to help readers understand the importance and significance of the various research articles. You make choices about which studies to include, then explain how the findings have been established and what areas of controversy remain. Interpret the existing research for your readers—help them to follow the logic of your outline. Notice that this assumes you started with an outline!
3. After doing all the background reading, you are the "expert" on that topic. Your readers, although likely educated people, may not be experts in that area. So write in a way that helps them follow the story. Explain any specialized language you use.

4. Look at the FAQs about APA style in the Closure section of this lab. Take a few minutes to read these sections before you begin to write, so that you can avoid mistakes.

5. Sometimes, in an effort to be scholarly, students fill their paper with "big words," but because the words are not the best choice for the thought they want to convey, they end up not making sense. "Being eloquent is not the same as using big words, and there is a delicious challenge to saying things simply, but with just the right words" (Locantore, 2001, p. 14). Choose your words to convey precisely what you mean rather than to impress your reader with your large vocabulary. Of course, if a big word says exactly what you mean, use it!

6. Look up the difference between affect and effect—these are frequently misused.

7. The word "data" is plural. You would say "The data *were* analyzed. . . ."

Practice using APA Style

This is an exercise in writing references in proper APA format. Write a reference page on the lines below using the following information. You may look in your textbook or in the *APA Publication Manual* for help.

Take the reference information given here and rewrite it in correct APA style. Watch for capitalization (or lack thereof), things that are italicized, hanging indentation, use of initials, and how page numbers are indicated. After you have rewritten these I'll show you the correct format. Don't peek until you've given it a try! Make any correction to your work that is needed.

1. This is a journal article written by E. Youngstrom, M. D. Weist, and K. E. Albus. It was published in 2003 in the American Journal of Community Psychology. You can find it on pages 115 through 129 in the 32nd volume of this journal. It is entitled "Exploring Violence Exposure, Stress, Protective Factors And Behavior Problems Among Inner-City Youth."

2. This is a chapter in an edited book. The chapter is entitled "National Institute of Mental Health and the Founding of the Field of Community Psychology," and was written by James G. Kelly. It is part of an edited book, p. 233–259, in which there are different authors for each chapter. The book, "Psychology and the National Institute of Mental Health: A Historical Analysis of Science, Practice, and Policy," was edited by Wade E. Pickren, Jr. and Stanley F. Schneider. It was published in 2005 by American Psychological Association, whose office is located in Washington, D.C.

(*Note:* Put citations in alphabetical order. Notice what word goes at the top center of the page.)

_____

_____

_____

_____

_____

_____

_____

_____

_____

_____

_____

    Correct versions of these references are given at the end of this lab manual.

Parts of an APA Style Paper

Now let's step back from the references and look at the formatting and organization of the overall paper. You are learning APA rules for preparing a manuscript. It will look a bit different from the typeset versions you have seen in journals. Each component is necessary for a complete research report. Each component is presented in a specified format. Below are parts of an APA paper in a scrambled order. Write them on several sheets of paper in correct order and correctly placed on the page. For example,

References	*Participants*
Title	Header
Author	*Procedure and Design*
Institution	
Running head: ABRIEVIATED TITLE	**Abstract**
Appendix	**Table 1**
Figure 1 [notice that figure titles are on a separate page from the actual figure]	**Method**
Discussion	**Results**
Title (repeated a second time)	*Materials*

some elements are centered on the page, while others are at the left margin. You may use your textbook and the *APA Publication Manual* (p. 306 and following) for help. If an element goes on a page by itself or must begin at the top of a new page, then use a new sheet of paper. For example, the title page has certain information on it, then the abstract begins on a new page. The introduction begins on a new page, but the method section doesn't. Notice which headings are italicized.

You will make use of headings in order to organize your paper and make it easier for the reader to follow. The *APA Publication Manual* uses specific types of headings for the various sections of the paper. They are identified by level number. You are most likely to use level 1, 3, or 4 headings. That being the case, identify the following as level 1, 3, or 4 headings. See your textbook or p. 113 of the *APA Publication Manual* for assistance. Notice which headings are italicized and/or followed by a period, where they are placed, and how they are used to organize the paper.

Method (level ___)

Materials (level ___)

Measures of working memory. (level ___) The "Count the Dots" task designed by Case (1984) was used. . . .

Putting It into Practice

Now it's time to put all this information to use, and produce your own literature review. First read the information in the *APA Publication Manual* on the pages indicated below under "FAQs about APA Style." Then read the section on "Writing It" found at http://depts.washington.edu/psywc/handouts.shtml. Scroll down and click on "Bem: Writing the empirical journal article." Read through the subsection entitled "Criticizing Previous Work." Also read the section entitled "Common Errors of Grammar and Usage."

Now . . . read the articles you've collected on your topic, develop an outline, and begin writing. Make sure you know when your literature review is due, and write early enough to go through several drafts before your due date.

Closure

FAQs about APA Style

The page numbers refer to the 5th edition of the *Publication Manual of the American Psychological Association*.

 Online help: http://core.ecu.edu/psyc/wuenschk/APA.htm

Questions

1. Where can I find a sample of a complete manuscript? p. 306 ff.
2. How do I do the reference page? p. 219 ff., examples begin on p. 239.
3. How do I list citations within my paper? p. 207 ff.
4. How do I use et al.? Do I have to write out all the authors' names each time I cite them? p. 208, p. 240.
5. How do I correctly cite a direct quote? p. 85 and p. 117–118
6. How do I type the different levels of headings? p. 113
7. How do I type numbers in my paper (spelled out or using numerals)? p. 122 ff
8. How do I cite a secondary source (i.e., something that was cited in a paper I read, but I have not read the original source)? p. 247
9. How do I cite an electronic source? p. 268 ff—also check http://www.apsu.edu/~lesterj/cyber4.htm.

Other useful sites:

http://www.waldenu.edu/acad-rsrcs/writing-center/rules.html (Effective Writing)

http://www.bedfordstmartins.com/online/citex.html (APA style for electronic sources; make sure you use the rules for APA style.)

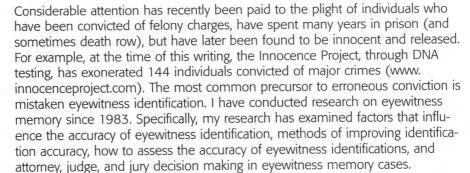

Descriptive and Inferential Statistics

Psychology and Law

DR. BRIAN CUTLER

Considerable attention has recently been paid to the plight of individuals who have been convicted of felony charges, have spent many years in prison (and sometimes death row), but have later been found to be innocent and released. For example, at the time of this writing, the Innocence Project, through DNA testing, has exonerated 144 individuals convicted of major crimes (www. innocenceproject.com). The most common precursor to erroneous conviction is mistaken eyewitness identification. I have conducted research on eyewitness memory since 1983. Specifically, my research has examined factors that influence the accuracy of eyewitness identification, methods of improving identification accuracy, how to assess the accuracy of eyewitness identifications, and attorney, judge, and jury decision making in eyewitness memory cases.

The methodology of this research involves simulations. For example, students are exposed to a simulated crime, such as a videotaped enactment of a crime or a staged theft during a class lecture. Students then serve as mock-witnesses and at a later time attempt to identify the perpetrator from a photoarray. In some experiments, I systematically manipulated the conditions under which the event was witnessed or the manner in which the photoarray was presented to the witnesses. Although crime simulation research is somewhat unrealistic, this methodology provides many important benefits that I could not get from studying actual crimes. For example, I can repeat a crime simulation many times to obtain a large sample (even hundreds) of eyewitnesses. I can hold most variables constant, while only manipulating factors of interest to me. Also, unlike an actual crime, I know the identity of the perpetrator with complete certainty, so I can determine for sure whether identifications are accurate or inaccurate. This research has revealed some very interesting results. For example, eyewitnesses shown sequential photoarrays (individual photos, one at a time) are much less likely to make a false identification than eyewitnesses shown the more traditional, simultaneously presented photoarrays (viewing all photos at the same time). Subtle differences in the manner in which eyewitnesses are instructed about the photoarray can greatly increase the likelihood of false identifications. It is very gratifying to see that this research and similar research by my colleagues in the field has led to positive changes in the criminal justice system. Several states, for example, New Jersey and North Carolina, have recently issued recommendations for how police should conduct identification tests. These recommendations relied heavily on eyewitness research, and, if implemented, we should see fewer mistaken identifications and erroneous convictions in the future.

Assignment

The purpose of this lab is to distinguish between descriptive and inferential statistics, to review the concept of statistical significance, to review how to use SPSS to calculate these statistics, and to identify this information on an SPSS output. Turn in: SPSS output and the answers to the questions asked in the "Closure" section below.

Topic

Children's eyewitness memory

Target Article

Nathanson, R., & Saywitz, K. J. (2003). The effects of the courtroom context on children's memory and anxiety. *Journal of Psychiatry and Law, 31*(1), 67–98.

Children's memory seems to be sensitive to context; they remember better in familiar, more comfortable settings. This study measured the memory and anxiety level (operationalized as heart rate) of 8 to 10-year-old children in two different settings: a mock courtroom and a small, private room. Children interviewed in the courtroom had greater heart rate variability, indicating stress, and poorer recall than children interviewed in the smaller room.

Descriptive vs. Inferential Statistics

We're going to look at two categories of statistical information for a set of data—descriptive and inferential. Descriptive statistics—no surprise here—describe the characteristics of a set of data. We're going to look at a measure of central tendency (the mean) and dispersion from the mean (the standard deviation). Inferential statistics allow us to infer something about the relation between groups or variables. They are used to determine whether group means or counts are significantly different, or whether two variables are significantly related to each other. If you use the word "significant" about data, you should have some type of inferential statistics to support your claim.

In our data set, we are comparing the number of correct facts recalled by children in two different contexts. Higher numbers indicate greater correct recall. Children's recall was assessed under two different conditions, once in the courtroom and once in a small, informal room. Good design requires that the order in which each child was tested be counterbalanced. That means that some children were tested first in the courtroom followed by the small room, whereas others began in the small room and moved to the courtroom. Notice, however, that each child was tested in both conditions. We could have tested different children in the two settings; in this case we opted to test the same children twice.

FYI

Note that all "canned" data sets in this lab manual were made up by the author, and did not come from the study described in the target article.

Setting Up the SPSS Data File*

1. Open SPSS. You'll see a box that asks "What would you like to do?"
2. Click *Type in data*
3. and *OK*. Now you have a blank spreadsheet.
4. Let's start by labeling the variables. In the bottom-left corner click the tab that says *Variable View*. Next to the number 1 enter "courtroom" then, "small_room" next to the number 2.
5. Just so I'll remember later, I enter a description of each variable under *label*. That way I'll know later, exactly, what I meant by each variable name. It also helps you interpret the output of SPSS as you'll see below.
6. Now click the tab that says *data view*. Type in these numbers.

courtroom	small_room
15.00	14.00
12.00	13.00
9.00	10.00
3.00	4.00

*All SPSS instructions are summarized in Appendix 2.

courtroom	small_room
6.00	5.00
12.00	14.00
10.00	10.00
8.00	10.00
4.00	6.00
17.00	19.00
6.00	8.00
8.00	6.00
2.00	3.00
9.00	10.00
14.00	15.00
21.00	22.00
5.00	7.00
3.00	4.00
8.00	8.00
9.00	11.00

In my experience you can never save your data too often.

1. Save by clicking *File* in the top-left corner
2. then *Save as*
3. Specify the drive and file name you want, then click *Save*. Thereafter you can simply click *save* or the save icon, if you'd like to complete the process more quickly.

Finding Descriptive Statistics

Now we'll use descriptive statistics to get an idea of the characteristics of our data.

1. Click *Analyze*
2. *Descriptive statistics*
3. *Descriptives*
4. Move the two variables into the variable box by highlighting each and clicking the arrow to the right.
5. When they have both been moved, click *OK*. This will produce the following information:

Descriptive Statistics					
	N	Minimum	Maximum	Mean	Std. Deviation
children's memory in courtroom setting	20	2.00	21.00	9.0500	4.97864
children's memory in small room setting	20	3.00	22.00	9.9500	5.06250
Valid N (listwise)	20				

See how, instead of the somewhat cryptic variable name, SPSS has provided the label for that variable? This is the information I typed in under the "label" column in variable view. From this table we know the sample size (N), the smallest and largest values for each variable, along with its mean and standard deviation. Recall that the standard deviation is the extent to which, on average, the scores differ from the mean. Large standard deviations mean more spread in the scores; small deviations indicate less spread. It is easier to compare two means when their standard deviations are similar.

Inferential Statistics

Now we know that the two settings produced different average recall, but how do we know if they are different enough to say that one setting prompted better (significantly greater) recall? So far we <u>don't</u> know, and can't make any statements about whether the differences are significant. In order to do that, we must make use of the other statistical category, inferential statistics; without inferential statistics, all you have is your subjective opinion. Begin this section by reviewing the tutorial at http://www.wadsworth.com/ psychology_d/templates/student_resources/workshops/stat_workshp/ hypth_test/hypth_test_01.html.

We'll get into more details about two-group comparisons in a later lab. For now, just follow these instructions.

1. Click *Analyze*
2. *Compare means*
3. *Paired-samples T-test*
4. Click <u>both</u> variables <u>then</u> the right arrow to move them into the paired variables box.
5. Click *OK*. Your output will look like this:

T-Test

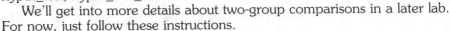

Paired Samples Statistics

		Mean	N	Std. Deviation	Std. Error Mean
Pair 1	children's recall in courtroom setting	9.0500	20	4.97864	1.11326
	children's recall in small room setting	9.9500	20	5.06250	1.13201

Paired Samples Correlations

		N	Correlation	Sig.
Pair 1	children's recall in courtroom setting & children's recall in small room setting	20	.973	.000

Paired Samples Test

		Paired Differences							
		Mean	Std. Deviation	Std. Error Mean	95% Confidence Interval of the Difference		t	df	Sig. (2-tailed)
					Lower	Upper			
Pair 1	children's recall in courtroom setting – children's recall in small room setting	–.90000	1.16529	.26057	–1.44537	–.35463	–3.454	19	.003

You got a recap of some of the descriptive information, followed by the correlation of our two variables. Ignore these boxes for now. The Paired Samples Test shows that the difference between the two means is significant, $t(19) = 3.45$, $p = .003$. How do I know the difference is significant? Look in the last cell that is labeled "Sig. (2-tailed)." If this value is less than .05, then I can say the difference between the means is significant. We now know that the difference is significant, but in order to know which condition was associated with greater recall, we'll have to look back at the descriptive statistics to see which mean was higher. When you report this information you'll include both the descriptive and inferential statistics.

What is So Special About "p < .05?"

What does $p < .05$ tell us? It means that you are taking less than 5% chance of making a Type 1 error. A Type 1 error is one in which the independent variable (IV) really-and-truly does not produce a difference in the population, but, based on your sample, you said there was a difference. A Type 2 error is when the IV really-and-truly does produce a difference in the population, but you said there wasn't one. Type 1 and 2 errors represent a trade-off; as one goes up, the other goes down. If you wanted to be really certain that you didn't make a Type 1 error, you could set the p value for a smaller number. In other words, you wouldn't call it significant, unless p was less than, for example, .01. However, when you decrease the chance of making a Type 1 error, you increase the chance of making a Type 2 error. What a choice! Convention has set the cutoff at .05.

Power

You know that you are more likely to get significant results if you have more rather than fewer participants, or if you use a repeated measures design. You may have come across studies that have examined the same topic—one study found that the IV made a significant difference while the other study found no effect of the IV.

Why is this? One reason may be that one or both studies didn't have enough participants. Large samples and repeated measures designs have greater "power." Power refers to the probability of correctly rejecting the null hypothesis. In other words, it is the probability that you were right when you decided, based on your sample, that the IV did produce a significant difference in the population.

So . . . what difference does power make to you? You want to give your experimental hypothesis a good chance of being supported, so you maximize the possibility that your statistical finding is significant. One way is to use a larger sample size. There are formulas and tables that can tell you how many participants you'll need to achieve a given power level—I'll leave the details for your statistics class. When you have a choice, go for a larger rather than a smaller sample size.

Closure

Reviewing what you've learned . . .

Why do researchers use inferential statistics? Why do you need anything besides descriptive statistics?

_____

_____

_____

_____

Why can't you look at two means, see that they are different, and decide that the difference is significant?

_____

_____

_____

_____

What do you know about the difference between two means when p is less than .05?

_____

_____

_____

_____

Why do most scientists use $p < .05$ (instead of some other value) as the criteria to determine significance?

_____

_____

_____

_____

How does the p value relate to Type I and Type II error?

_____

_____

_____

_____

Part II

Research Designs—
Nonexperimental

Correlational Design

Industrial/Organizational Psychology

DR. KIM BUCH

Industrial/Organizational (I/O) psychology is a broad subdiscipline within psychology that focuses on people and processes in the workplace. I/O psychologists apply the principles of psychology to the workplace in order to enhance organizational effectiveness and individual satisfaction, while maximizing the fit between the worker and the work environment. Topics in the field include those related to human resources management (HRM), such as employee recruitment and selection, performance appraisal, and employee training and development. Other topics include those related to organizational behavior (OB), such as leadership, employee motivation, work attitudes, and team and organizational development. I/O research can focus on any of these topics, and may include studies that seek to understand and improve work behaviors and attitudes, studies to test the impact of HR or organizational interventions on work outcomes, or studies which explore work roles and relationships.

The next seven labs can be divided into two groups: nonexperimental methods and experimental methods. What is the difference between the two? Experimental studies use random assignment to groups and have an independent variable (IV) that is manipulated. Some research questions simply can't be studied using an experimental design, so a nonexperimental one is chosen. Correlational and survey designs are nonexperimental methods frequently used. The third lab on nonexperimental designs introduces some less common nonexperimental designs. This is followed by four labs involving experimental designs.

Assignment

Today you will set up a data file, run and interpret a correlational analysis, and write a short results section for the analysis. Turn in: output of correlational analysis and short results section describing the results.

Topic

Sleep and work safety

Target Articles

Leger, D., Guilleminault, C., Bader, G., Levy, E., & Paillard, M. (2002). Medical and socio-professional impact of insomnia. *Journal of Sleep and Sleep Disorders Research, 25*(6), 621–625.

Cavallo, A., Ris, M. D., & Succop, P. (2003). The night float paradigm to decrease sleep deprivation: Good solution or a new problem? *Ergonomics, 46*(7), 653–663.

The first study listed above compared people with insomnia (but no depression) with good sleepers. People with severe insomnia demonstrated a number of health- and work-related problems. They were more likely to have medical problems, go to the doctor, be hospitalized, and take more medication. At work they were more likely to be absent, had difficulty with concentrating and carrying out their jobs, and were more likely to report accidents at work. This study compared means of two groups (a two-group design—we'll get to that later).

The second study examined the impact of a "night float rotation" on the sleep, mood, and performance of medical residents. "Night float rotation" is a work schedule in which the individual works at night but has no daytime duties (as compared to being on duty for, say, 24 hours at a time). Even though the residents had enough time during the day to sleep, they got fewer hours of sleep than they did while on a typical daytime rotation. Measures of fatigue during the night float rotation were correlated with measures of attention. Greater sleepiness was associated with more errors of attention.

Do Sleepier People Have More Accidents at Work?

In the second study described above, sleepiness when on a nighttime shift was associated with errors of attention. Impaired attention could cause more accidents and errors when working. For this lab, we're going to examine the relationship between average hours of sleep and number of accidents on the job. We're going to compare the rank-ordering of these two variables. We want to know if the rank-ordering varies in a systematic way. We are predicting that people who get the most sleep tend to have the fewest accidents. To do this we will measure two variables—amount of sleep and number of accidents—for each participant and then correlate the variables.

 First of all, let's review the use of correlational designs and the correlation statistic. Read the tutorial at http://www.wadsworth.com/psychology_ d/templates/student_resources/workshops/stat_workshp/correlation/ correlation_01.html. Now go to http://noppa5.pc.helsinki.fi/koe/corr/ cor7.html to review what scatter plots for positive and negative, strong and weak correlations look like.

Entering and Analyzing the Data

Now you're ready to do your own correlational analysis. Enter the following data (or the data collected from you and your classmates; see "If You Wish . . ." below) into SPSS. The variable labeled "avg_slp" is the average hours slept at night and "accident" indicates the number of accidents over the previous 12 months.

avg_slp	accident
7.00	2.00
6.00	4.00
4.00	3.00
7.00	3.00
4.00	6.00
5.00	6.00
4.00	7.00
9.00	2.00
9.00	4.00
8.00	3.00
7.00	4.00
4.00	5.00
6.00	3.00
9.00	1.00
8.00	2.00
5.00	5.00
6.00	4.00
8.00	5.00
5.00	6.00
7.00	6.00

Run the correlational analysis. Click

1. *Analyze*
2. *Correlate*
3. *Bivariate*

4. Highlight the names of the two variables and click the arrow to the right to move them into the variable box.
5. Now click *OK*

Your output should look like this:

Correlations

		AVG_SLP	ACCIDENT
AVG_SLP	Pearson Correlation	1	−.634*
	Sig. (2-tailed)	.	.003
	N	20	20
ACCIDENT	Pearson Correlation	−.634*	1
	Sig. (2-tailed)	.003	.
	N	20	20

*Correlation is significant at the 0.01 level (2-tailed)

Notice that we are using the Pearson correlation. This is used when both variables are interval or ratio scale measures. There are other measures that can be used when one or both variables use another scale.

The correlation between hours slept and number of accidents is −.634, the sample size was 20, and the significance level is .003. Is this a significant correlation? ___ The fact that it is negative means that people who get more sleep have (more or fewer) accidents. _____ Does this support our prediction? ___

Reporting the Results

Now we're going to write a very short results section about these data. Because this may be your first try at a results section, I'll give you an example.

Results

The average hours slept by participants was correlated with the number of accidents they had reported during the previous 12 months. The two variables were significantly correlated, $r(20) = -.634$, $p = .003$, indicating that participants who averaged more hours of sleep at night tended to have fewer accidents.

Notice several things here. You told the reader what statistics were used, what the variables were, that they were significantly correlated, then you backed that up by reporting the statistics. The *r* and *p* are both lower case and italicized, and the sample size is indicated after the *r*. Finally, you helped the reader understand what the significant statistics meant.

Now . . . close this lab manual, look at the SPSS printout, and write a short results section. When you are done compare what you wrote to the example above. Did you include all the relevant information? Did you report the statistics using proper format? Did you explain the correlation to the reader?

If You Wish to Collect Your Own Data

If you'd like to analyze data generated by your class, use the chart below to keep track of how much time you slept the night before an exam. The two variables correlated will be number of hours slept and your grade in the exam. What would you predict about a correlation between these two variables? Bear in mind that staying up at night to cram for a test is not a productive study strategy for two reasons. We know that distributed practice (smaller study sessions over several study periods) produces better recall than does massed practice (one intensive study session), and sleep deprivation may decrease your ability to do things like recall, pay attention, solve problems, organize your thoughts, and so on.

Hours slept the night before the exam: _____

Grade on exam: _____

Now you need to include your data with that of your other classmates. Pass around a spread sheet and have everyone (anonymously) fill in his or her numbers. Enter these data into an SPSS file and analyze as described above.

	Hours slept	*Grade*
Person 1	_____	_____
Person 2	_____	_____
Person 3	_____	_____ . . . and so on . . .

Closure

Correlations do . . .

1. compare the nature of association between two variables, indicating whether or not there is a relationship.
2. indicate whether the relationship is strong, weak, or nonexistent, and whether the factors measured vary in the same direction (positive correlations) or opposite directions (negative correlations).

Correlations do not . . .

1. compare group means.
2. indicate cause and effect. Variable A *may* have caused Variable B, but it is just as possible that Variable B caused Variable A, or that there is some other variable, C, out there that is causing both A and B. We can't tell on the basis of the correlation.

Surveys

Health Psychology

DR. VIRGINIA GIL-RIVAS

Health psychology is interested in understanding the interaction between biological characteristics (e.g., genes), psychological (e.g., stress, mood), and social factors (e.g., culture, family relationships, socioeconomic status) and their contribution to health and illness. Research in this area focuses on health promotion and illness prevention and treatment. Health promotion efforts involve designing programs that encourage people to engage in behaviors, such as regular physical exercise, maintaining a balanced diet and healthy weight. Prevention efforts focus on reducing individuals' risk of developing an illness or engaging in behaviors that can lead to illness (e.g., smoking, alcohol and substance abuse). Treatment efforts focus on developing interventions that limit negative impact of illness on the physical and psychological well-being of individuals and their families (e.g., relaxation, biofeedback, cognitive behavioral therapy).

Some of the common topics examined in health psychology include: (1) the impact of stress on physiological processes (e.g., immune function); (2) the association between stress and illness; (3) the impact of chronic and serious illnesses (e.g., diabetes, cardiovascular disease, cancer, HIV); (4) health-related behaviors (e.g., smoking, substance use, exercise, sleep, diet); (5) personality (e.g., Type A behavior, self-efficacy); (6) social and cultural influences (e.g., media, social relationships); (7) adherence/compliance to medical treatment; and (8) the doctor-patient relationship.

Assignment

In today's lab you will design and pilot-test a survey intended to measure stress and number of visits to health care providers by college students, collect data using this survey, then examine the descriptive statistics of the data as well as correlate the two variables. Canned data will be provided for those instructors who do not want students to collect data. You will write a short introduction and results section to a lab report on the topic of stress and health. Turn in: copy of the survey you developed (or examples of questions you might include in such a survey), introduction and results sections for either the data you collect or the canned data.

Topic

Connections between stress and physical health among college students

Target Article

Hamrick, H., Cohen, S., & Rodriguez, M. S. (2002). Being popular can be healthy or unhealthy: Stress, social network diversity, and incidence of upper respiratory infection. *Health Psychology, 21*(3), 294–298.

Popular people, or those who have lots of social contacts, are exposed to more germs than are people who don't have as many social contacts. Does that suggest that they will be more likely to get sick? These authors measured social network diversity and stressful life events in college students, then interviewed their participants weekly for 12 weeks, recording how many upper respiratory infections they contracted during that time. They found that the answer to whether or not the popular people got sick more often was "it depends." They did become sick more often if they had a high stress score, but not if they reported low stress. In other words, it seemed that stress weakened their resistance to germs, making them more likely to succumb to the germs to which they were exposed.

Surveys can be used to help understand the characteristics of a population, or can collect data that can be analyzed in various ways. For this example, let's assume you are going to use a survey to collect information about perceived stress (how stressed the participants feel themselves to be) and how healthy they are. We will use a correlation to compare the rank order of amount or degree of stress with degree of health.

Types of Survey Questions

Questions on surveys can take several forms. They can be open-ended or closed-ended. An example of an open-ended question might be . . .

What concerns (if any) do you have about the amount of alcohol you drink?

_____

Closed-ended questions limit participants' responses. These are examples of closed-ended survey items:

Do you smoke currently? ____ yes   ____ no

When you do well on a test, is it because (check one) . . .

____A. you are smart in that subject?

____B. you worked hard studying for the test?

____C. the teacher likes you?

____D. you were lucky that day?

____E. other reason

When you go to your first class of the day, how sleepy are you usually? Circle the number that best describes you.

_____1_____2_____3_____4_____5_____6_____7_____8_____9_____

Very sleepy   Neither sleepy   Not at all
                                 nor alert   sleepy

Open-ended questions are good for getting answers unique to each participant. However, you then will have to develop some way to convert that information to numbers if you wish to do some type of quantitative analysis.

Developing the Survey

First review characteristics of good survey items (this is probably described in your textbook), then brainstorm in small groups to come up with survey items that measure stress and/or health. Create your measures so that high scores indicate greater stress and more health concerns (i.e., poorer health) respectively.

Measuring Stress

Stress can be operationalized as physiological measures such as blood pressure, heartrate, galvanic skin response, or respiration rate, or it can be measured in terms of recent stressful life events (such as marriage, death of a loved one), or daily hassles (such as feeling annoyed or frustrated). For purposes of this lab you may devise your own method of measuring stress, or you may choose to use the survey of life events in the article cited below. This instrument was chosen because it was developed to tap life events common to college students. Alternatively, you can write your own measure of perceived stress.

Renner, M. J., & Scott, M. R. (1998). A life stress instrument of classroom use. *Teaching of Psychology, 25*(1), 46–48.

Health

You can operationalize this as the number of visits to health care providers during the last 12 months (you'll need to specify what you include in the term "health care provider" for your participants), or you can develop other survey items that can be used to generate a health score. For example, you may ask how many colds a person has had, how many prescription medicines have been used, or some other indicator of health, and then add up the numbers to produce the health score.

Once you have a number of survey items you think will get the information you want, pilot test them on a few people (similar to those who will be your participants) to identify any problems with the items. Were some of them confusing? Unclear? Did they allow for all possible responses? Ask the pilot testers to comment on each item. Either fix or eliminate poor items.

If You Wish To Collect Your Own Data

When you are satisfied with the final survey, identify whom you wish to include in your study. Decide on a strategy for collecting the data. Remember you are seeking personal information from your participants, so give them the opportunity to read and sign an informed consent form (an example is given at the end of this lab), and come up with a way to ensure their anonymity. One way to do this is to have two boxes with slits on top. Participants can put their surveys and consent forms in different boxes. They might want to fold them up first, then shake the box after putting in their information to mix up the contents (making it harder to associate a consent form with that person's survey). Perhaps you can come up with an even better way to keep your participants' responses anonymous. If this is a class project, you can either collect data from all class members, or have class members collect data from people outside the class. Decide how many participants will be recruited by each class member. Each person can use the data collection form below to record his or her results, then bring the results to class and pool them to make one large data set. Enter the data into SPSS (or enter the canned data provided below), label the variables, then run the analyses indicated.

Data collection form:

	Stress score	Health score
Participant 1	_____	_____
Participant 2	_____	_____
Participant 3	_____	_____ . . . and so on . . .

Canned Data

For these data, assume that the stress measure can range from 100 to 3000, and that higher numbers indicate greater stress. The health measure is the number of sickness-related visits to health care providers in the last 12 months, and ranged from 0 to 24. Higher numbers, therefore, indicate more instances of sickness, and therefore, worse health. Enter the data as you did before.

stress	health
565.00	12.00
288.00	3.00
144.00	2.00
1583.00	10.00
994.00	6.00
187.00	3.00
255.00	3.00
2004.00	14.00
2299.00	11.00
634.00	2.00
951.00	4.00
249.00	9.00
761.00	.00
267.00	3.00
852.00	5.00
147.00	.00
369.00	6.00
963.00	7.00
741.00	6.00
852.00	7.00

Analyses

First let's "eyeball" the data by looking at some of the descriptive statistics.

1. Click *Analyze, Descriptive statistics*
2. then highlight each variable and click the arrow to move it into the variable box,
3. then click *OK*

Descriptive Statistics					
	N	Minimum	Maximum	Mean	Std. Deviation
stress	20	144.00	2299.00	755.2500	607.62635
health	20	.00	14.00	5.6500	3.93734
valid N (listwise)	20				

You see that you have the sample size, the minimum and maximum scores reported by your participants, the mean score of each variable, and the standard deviation of that score (i.e., the extent to which, on average, the scores differ from the mean).

Now use the steps presented in the previous lab to correlate these two variables.

Correlations		stress	health
stress	Pearson Correlation	1	.677*
	Sig. (2-tailed)	.	.001
	N	20	20
health	Pearson Correlation	.677*	1
	Sig. (2-tailed)	.001	.
	N	20	20

*Correlation is significant at the 0.01 level

This time you have a positive correlation. Is it significant? What does the positive correlation indicate about the relation between stress and health (remember high scores indicate more stress and more health problems)?

Results Section

This time we're going to add the descriptive information to the results section. Begin by indicating the sample size, mean and standard deviation for each variable, then report the correlation. Use the example from the last lab to help you report the correlation. Write the results section before you look at the example below.

_____

_____

_____

_____

_____

_____

_____

_____

_____

Results

Twenty participants completed the survey indicating the number of stressful life events they had experienced over the previous 12 months (M = 755.25, SD = 607.63, range 144–2299) as well as the number of visits made to health care providers during the same time period (M = 5.65, SD = 3.94, range 0–14). The two variables were significantly correlated, $r(20)$ = .677, p = .001, indicating that participants who reported more stressful life events during the previous 12 months had made more visits to health care providers during the same period of time.

Compare what you wrote to the example given here. Did you include all the important information? Did you italicize letters used to report statistics?

Producing the Abbreviated Lab Report

Write an introduction and results section of a lab report to turn in to your instructor. Ask your instructor what types of sources are appropriate for you to use (e.g., textbooks, articles found on PsycINFO). An introduction is essentially a literature review, with the purpose and hypothesis for the study described at the end. Set up your literature review to move from a general discussion of the research topic to a more detailed look at the specific topic to be addressed by this study, then add on a paragraph or two describing the purpose and hypothesis for this study. Next include the results section you wrote above (with any corrections or improvements needed, of course).

Closure

In most cases, anyone who wants to conduct research should (and often must) first have his or her research proposal approved by an IRB (refer back to Lab 3 on Ethics). The research you are doing for this class, however, is being undertaken for learning purposes rather than research purposes. Is it acceptable to collect data without IRB approval when it is for learning purposes only? Although I don't know the position the IRB at your institution takes, here is how one institution has settled this question: http://www.legal.uncc.edu/policies/ps-63.html, see Section III.

Your instructor will guide you regarding any required approval for data collection. Whether you are required to do so or not, it is always a good idea to use an informed consent form. Your participants should be told in advance what you will ask them, and know that they can quit whenever they like. The following page is an example of an informed consent form. Your instructor may require that you use a different format or include different statements. This is a shorter version of what your IRB may require in a consent form. Replace the sections in italics with wording appropriate to your project.

Informed Consent Form

This experiment is being conducted by *Person Doe* as a class project for Research Methods at the *University of XYZ*. The experiment is under the supervision of *Dr. Doe* in the Department of Psychology. It deals with *your ability to recall words*. If you agree to participate, *I will read you a list of word pairs. I will then give you the first word from each pair and you will have to recall the word that goes with it.* The experiment should take *about ten minutes.*

Your participation in this experiment is voluntary and you are free to withdraw at any time without penalty, and remove any data that you have contributed. Your responses to the survey will be *anonymous [or confidential, depending on your procedure]*. This informed consent will be kept separate from your responses. The responses that you provide will be used by this student for the purpose of learning about research methodology, and will not be reported outside of the class. If you have any questions about the way you have been treated in this study or about how your data will be used, contact *Dr. Doe* at *xxx-xxx-xxxx*.

Thank you for your participation.

_____

I acknowledge that I am at least 18 years old and that the purposes and procedures of this experiment have been explained to me to my satisfaction. I understand that my participation is totally voluntary and that I am free to withdraw at any time with no penalty. Knowing this, I freely consent to participate.

Signed _____

Date _____

Other Nonexperimental Designs

Exercise and Sport Psychology

As is happening in other areas of psychology, Exercise and Sport Psychology is interdisciplinary because it involves concepts and theories that come from several areas of psychology (for example, social, physiological, clinical, development, and health just to name a few) as well as sport sciences. These psychologists might research such topics as what motivates athletes to persist at learning a sport or acquiring a skill, and, eventually, what motivates them to achieve distinction in that sport. They might study the psychological mechanisms involved in sports injury and rehabilitation. They may provide counseling to athletes, or examine which counseling techniques are most effective among athletes. Other topics could include methods for assessing talent, youth sports issues, what variables contribute to persistence in exercising, self-perceptions related to achieving, the development of expertise in a particular area, and the enhancement or self-regulation of one's performance. This area of psychology has been around since the 1980s. The Web site for this division can be found at http://www.psyc.unt.edu/apadiv47/index.html.

This information is based on a description of Exercise and Sport Psychology, a division of the APA. This information can be found at http://www.psyc.unt.edu/apadiv47/about_purposeandgoals.html

Assignment

The purpose of this lab is to familiarize you with some additional nonexperimental methods and give you the opportunity to make an oral presentation. Instead of turning in written work, you and your team will teach the rest of the class about a particular type of nonexperimental method. Pointers for giving an oral presentation are included at the end of this lab.

Topic

The nature of the imagery used during exercise

Target Article

Giacobbi, P. R. Jr., Hausenblas, H. A., Fallon, E. A., & Hall, C. A. (2003). Even more about exercise imagery: A grounded theory of exercise imagery. *Journal of Applied Sport Psychology, 15*(2), 160–175.

Can you use imagery to improve or sustain your exercise? What sort of mental images might you use? Rather than comparing several groups for some dependent variable, or correlating two variables, these authors used the nonexperimental research method of grounded theory to understand what sort of imagery regular exercisers used during exercise. They asked 16 female exercisers to describe the content of the imagery they produced while they exercised. Using strategies of analysis specific to grounded theory (one of the nonexperimental methods to be covered in this lab), they identified eight themes of the imagery. Several themes referred to the exercise activity and surroundings: techniques of exercise, the context in which it occurred, aerobic routines, and competitive outcomes. Other themes involved physical or emotional well-being: appearance, fitness/health, and emotions/feelings. The participants indicated that appearance and fitness goals were important to the continuation of exercise.

Work Plan

Your instructor will assign each class member to one of six teams. Each team is charged with learning about a specific nonexperimental method. They are to put together information about it and examples of studies using this method. They should give examples of the types of research questions that could be addressed using that method. They then decide how their team's report on that method is to be organized and what each team member will present. Each group will be responsible for a _____-minute presentation on your assigned topic to be given _____ (date). You choose how to divide up the tasks and in what order to present the information. You may draw material from your text, other textbooks, journals, the Web sites below and any other Web sites you find to be helpful. Do a PsycINFO search on these methods. Each person in the group must speak for at least _____ minutes, so once you have your information decide who will talk about each part. Even if you use notes to help you remember your material, try to know your part well enough so as not to read it entirely.

Team Assignments

I. Qualitative research

http://www.qualitativeresearch.uga.edu/QualPage/
http://tortoise.oise.utoronto.ca/~skarsten/research/QRsites.html#
    QUALITATIVE%20RESEARCH
http://www.analytictech.com/mb870/introtoGT.htm

A. Grounded theory

http://bri.bbwebmedia.com/research/research_methods.html#qualitative
http://www.groundedtheory.com/
http://www.ed.uiuc.edu/EPS/PES-Yearbook/95_docs/haig.html

II. Observational designs (may be qualitative or quantitative)
  A. Case studies

http://psychclassics.yorku.ca/Broca/perte-e.htm
http://www.nova.edu/ssss/QR/QR3-3/tellis2.html

Look in an introductory psychology text book and a child psychology textbook. How did Freud and Piaget use case studies to build their theories? If you can get a copy through your library or inter-library loan, read about a case study of a woman who believed she was extremely ugly:

Holt, D. J., Phillips, K. A., Shapiro, E. R., & Becker, A. E. (2003). "My face is my fate": Biological and psychosocial approaches to the treatment of a woman with obsessions and delusions. *Harvard Review of Psychiatry, 11*(3), 142–154.

B. Naturalistic observational studies

http://www.gpc.edu/~bbrown/psyc1501/methods/obs.htm
http://www.urich.edu/~pli/teaching/psy200/ResearchMethods/
    ObservationalResearch.html
http://www.orientpacific.com/observational-techniques.htm
http://www.a2xconsulting.com/observational_research.html

C. Ethnography

http://www.uccb.ns.ca/mikmaq/ethnog.html
http://lucy.ukc.ac.uk/EthnoAtlas/Hmar/Cult_dir/Culture.7853
http://writing.colostate.edu/guides/research/observe/com3a1.cfm

III. Interrupted time-series design

http://www.nhtsa.dot.gov/people/outreach/safedige/WINTER96/Alcohol/
    New_Mexico.html
http://www.mdrc.org/Reports99/EstimatingImpacts/InteruptedTimePaper.
    html#ABSTRACT

Closure

*How to Give an Effective Oral Presentation**

I. Topic should be appropriate for the speaker, the audience, the occasion and setting, and the time limit.

II. Analyze the audience's needs, existing knowledge, demographics, and size. Gather audience-related information.

III. Gathering material for your speech
   A. Select and use support material that clarifies, justifies, or generates interest.
   B. Your material should be varied, relevant, accurate, from objective sources, authoritative, and clear.
   C. Use visual aids when appropriate.

IV. Constructing your speech
   A. Organize your material. For example, you can organize it in chronological order, by topics, or using a problem-solution format.
   B. Introduction
      i.   Start with an attention-getter such as a statistic, quotation, story, question, illustration, or humor.
      ii. State the importance of the material you will present.
      iii. Preview what you will say.
      iv. Offer credibility for your statements (what is the source of your material?).
   C. Conclusion
      i.   Signal the end is coming.
      ii. Summarize your points or main ideas.
      iii. End with something that gives closure, such as a challenge, closing remarks, something that ties back into the introduction.

V. Presenting your speech
   A. Dealing with anxiety before you begin to speak
      i.   Know what to expect.
      ii. Choose a topic you care about.
      iii. Analyze the audience.
      iv. Rehearse thoroughly—practice.
      v.   Use mental imagery to visualize yourself giving a successful presentation.
   B. Controlling anxiety during your speech
      i.   Get settled; pause and get organized before you begin.
      ii. Survey (look at) the audience.
      iii. Never apologize for being nervous.
      iv. Remain task-oriented.
      v.   Slow down; avoid a rapid delivery.

---

*Based on uncopyrighted material presented in a training video produced by the Department of Communications, UNC Charlotte.

C. Rehearsal
    i. Use notes, but don't read.
    ii. Rehearse the speech as a whole.
    iii. Rehearse under similar conditions.
    iv. Rehearse in front of a full-length mirror.
    v. Make changes as needed.
    vi. Rehearse as often as necessary.
    vii. Rehearse with visual aids.

D. Delivering your speech
    i. Verbal pointers: slow down in general, but vary your speech as appropriate; make sure everyone can hear you easily; pronounce things correctly (look it up if you're not sure); insert pauses to emphasize points; avoid verbal "filler."
    ii. Nonverbal pointers: make eye contact; use good posture; use movement or gestures when it helps to make a point, but don't be distracting.

Research Designs—
Experimental

Two-Group Designs

Cognitive Psychology

Cognitive psychology is the study of anything your mind does. It studies topics such as attention and perception, memory, language, problem solving, decision making, consciousness, knowledge representation, creativity, and intelligence. It often studies these processes under controlled, laboratory conditions, but many people also study these topics in natural settings (such as home, the work place, or even grocery stores!). As is true in other areas of psychology, cognitive scientists may study basic processes (such as how attention works) or applications of cognition (such as how to predict who will make a good fighter pilot by measuring attention abilities). One branch of cognition, called Human Factors, studies human-machine interactions. Cognitive psychology has been expanding lately into a broader field called cognitive science. Cognitive science includes professionals from information technology, philosophy, linguistics, anthropology, and neurosciences as well as psychology. These professionals may collaborate to study the topics mentioned above as they relate to artificial intelligence, or to examine their neurological bases.

Assignment

Now we arrive at the simplest experimental design. You will compare your recall of words encoded either shallowly or deeply (based on Craik &

Lockhart's Levels of Processing). The same data will be analyzed in two different scenarios—once as if it had been a between subjects design (different people in each of two groups) and once as if it had been a repeated measures design (the same people tested twice). Analyzing the same data in two different designs will help you see how different designs can produce different statistical outcomes. Turn in: method and results sections of a lab report.

Your instructor may also want to assign you an intermediate draft of your final paper that includes the introduction and method section of your individual project. See specific instructions in Appendix 1.

Topic

The effect of shallow and deep encoding on memory

Target Articles

Craik, F. I., & Lockhart, R. S. (1972). Levels of processing: A framework for memory research. *Journal of Verbal Learning and Verbal Behavior, 11*(6), 671–684.

Craik, F. I., & Tulving, E. (1975). Depth of processing and the retention of words in episodic memory. *Journal of Experimental Psychology: General, 104*(3), 268–294.

In 1972, Craik and Lockhart proposed a theory of memory called "levels of processing" (also called depth of processing). This suggested that not all long-term memories are created equally; some have been deeply encoded, making them more durable and easier to recall, whereas others were encoded shallowly, and are therefore less likely to endure or be retrieved. Depth of encoding refers to the amount of meaningfulness used when encoding a memory and the extent to which the input is elaborated (connected to other memories). If you study a list of words by thinking of a specific example of each word, then you are forced to think about the meaning of the word as well as relating it to your existing memories, and it is therefore encoded more deeply. On the other hand, if you study a list of words focusing on whether each word contains any letters with curved lines, then the words are encoded shallowly because you don't necessarily access the meaning of the words or relate them to any other memories.

Background

For more information on levels of processing, see the following Web sites:

http://www.ship.edu/~ambart/PSY_325/Levels.htm
http://www.smarterkids.org/research/paper1.asp (This is an application of the theory)
http://www.alleydog.com/cognotes/memmodels.html

Now review independent vs. repeated measures designs in your text-book or at http://www.wadsworth.com/psychology_d/templates/student_resources/workshops/stat_workshp/ttest_betwn/ttest_betwn_01.html.

Be the Participant

Let's begin by serving as your own participants. Someone will serve as the experimenter. The experimenter will read the instructions in bold print below. You will record your own data, then compile it into one large data set. (Alternatively, you will use the canned data below.) To assign partici-pants to either group 1 or 2, flip a coin for each person, and give him or her Group 1 instructions if heads, Group 2 instructions if tails.

Materials and Procedure

I am going to read two lists of words to you. I want you to analyze the words by following the instructions assigned to your group. Use the "yes" and "no" columns on the next page to keep your tally and record your recall. We'll do this for each list, with different instruc-tions for each list (see instructions below). I will then tell you how to score the data. Each group has a different order of instructions. When you fill in the tally marks and write down your recall, make sure it is under the column of the instructions you used for that list.

After scoring, we'll enter the data into a spreadsheet. Make sure that when you report your score you do so in <u>this</u> order, even if this was not the order of your instructions:

Instructions A	Instructions B
(double letter)	(concrete)

Read the list of words at a rate of about one per two seconds. Use a stopwatch or a watch with a seconds hand to help you keep a steady pace.

Follow instructions for your group's list . . .

1st list	2nd list
horse	carriage
cabbage	carrot
elephant	aunt
gold	red

1st list	2nd list
trout	dog
rabbit	house
uncle	mother
knee	Indian
duck	bass
memory	patient
brain	ankle
picnic	radio
grill	blue
earlobe	leaf

After each list, do a distractor task (such as counting backwards by 3s, starting with 369, or reciting the words to your school's alma mater) for about 30 seconds, then have participants write down all the words from that list they recall.

Have participants give themselves a point for each word correctly recalled from each of the lists. Write that number in the box next to the tally box. Have each person report recall for lists recalled under instructions A and B if they are willing to do so (no one is required to supply data). Alternatively, you can have each person turn in their recall anonymously, then you can compile their responses into one data file.

Levels of Processing Instructions
(Follow the instructions for either Group 1 or Group 2.)

GROUP 1:

1st list (A): Does the word contain any double letters (such as "book" or "called")? Mark a tally under yes or no for each word.
2nd list (B): Is the word concrete? Mark yes for concrete words like "bed" but no for abstract words like "liberty."

GROUP 2:

1st list (B): Is the word concrete? Mark yes for concrete words like "bed" but no for abstract words like "liberty."
2nd list (A): Does the word contain any double letters (such as "book" or "called")? Mark a tally under yes or no for each word.

Notice that the order of presentation of the instructions is counterbalanced (some people followed the "double letter" instructions on the first list, while the others followed the "concrete" instructions on the first list). This should be mentioned in the procedure section of your paper. Why did we do this?

Use the following form to record your data.

Levels of Processing Data

	Instructions A (double letter)		Instructions B (concrete word)		
	Yes	No	Yes	No	**First,** keep a yes/no tally for each word on each list . . .
Word 1					
Word 2					
Word 3					
Word 4					
Word 5					
Word 6					
Word 7					
Word 8					←
Word 9					
Word 10					
Word 11					
Word 12					
Word 13					
Word 14					
Word 15					
Word 16					

↓

. . . **then** write down as many words from each list as you can remember . . .

Recall for instructions A (double letter)   Recall for instructions B (concrete)

↓

. . . **finally,** make a record here of how many words you correctly recalled from each list. This is the information you will record on the class data file.

My total correct recall for . . . Instructions A (double letter) _____ Instructions B (concrete) _____

Collecting the Data

Set up a piece of paper so that each person can write down their recall under the two conditions. For example, you might pass around a paper on which two columns are indicated, and having enough lines for everyone in the class to enter their data. To improve confidentiality, you can let each person enter their data on any line they wish; they don't have to fill in the next available blank line. Your data sheet may look something like this . . .

Recall for double letter condition	*Recall for concrete/abstract condition*
1. _____	_____
2. _____	_____

. . . and so on.

Analyses

Within Subjects Design

First let's analyze your data using the design we actually utilized—repeated measures (also called within-subjects), in which the same people were tested in both conditions. I'll illustrate data entry and analysis using canned data, but you can follow the instructions using the data you collected if your instructor wants you to do so. To set up a data file for a repeated measures design you'll need one column for each level of the independent variable. In this case we have two levels, double letter and concrete.

doub_let	concrete
12.00	12.00
9.00	8.00
13.00	14.00
7.00	11.00
9.00	10.00
14.00	14.00
5.00	7.00
8.00	10.00
5.00	7.00
10.00	11.00
11.00	12.00
13.00	14.00
12.00	8.00
13.00	10.00
6.00	12.00
10.00	10.00
7.00	9.00
13.00	14.00
10.00	14.00
9.00	11.00

Because we have the same people in both groups, we can use the paired-samples *t*-test. Click

1. *Analyze*
2. *Compare means*
3. *Paired-samples t-test*
4. Highlight both variables then move them into the Paired Variables Box, then click *OK*.

Your output should look like this (with different numbers, of course, if you used your own data):

T-Test

Paired Samples Statistics

		Mean	N	Std. Deviation	Std. Error Mean
Pair 1	doub_let	9.8000	20	2.82097	.63079
	concrete	10.9000	20	2.35975	.52766

Paired Samples Correlations

		N	Correlation	Sig.
Pair 1	doub_let & concrete	20	.637	.003

Paired Samples Test

| | Paired Differences | | | | | | | |
| | | | | 95% Confidence Interval of the Difference | | | | |
		Mean	Std. Deviation	Std. Error Mean	Lower	Upper	t	df	Sig. (2-tailed)
Pair 1	doub_let concrete	−1.10000	2.24546	.50210	−2.15091	−0.04909	−2.191	19	.041

Is the difference in recall between the two conditions significant? Make sure you can locate the descriptive information, the values for *t*, *p*, and degrees of freedom. Here's one way to report this information.

Results

Data from the 20 participants were analyzed using a paired-samples *t*-test. Recall in the concrete condition (*M* = 10.0, *SD* = 2.36) was significantly higher than recall in the double letter condition (*M* = 9.8, *SD* = 2.82), *t*(19) = 2.19, *p* = .04. As predicted, deeper encoding produced greater recall.

Between Subjects Design

Now let's pretend. Pretend that we collected this data using a between-subjects design. In this scenario, 20 people were assigned to the double letter condition and 20 *different* people were assigned to the concrete condition. Now how many participants do you have?____ Since we have different people in the two conditions we must now use the independent-samples *t*-test. To set up a data file for this design you will need one column for the independent variable and one for the dependent variable. Since each participant was tested under only one condition, the first column is used here to identify each participant's group; let's use 1 to indicate the double letter condition and 2 to indicate the concrete condition. A few days from now you may not remember which condition was identified as 1 and which one as 2. Identify the meaning of those numbers by using the Values column of the Variable View. In Variable View, on the same line as the word "condition,"

1. Click the box under Values then click the small gray box that pops up in the right of that area.
2. Enter the value of 1 and the label "double letter" (you don't need the quotations marks), then click *Add*.
3. Follow the same steps to identify 2 as "concrete," then click *OK*. You can set up the recall column quickly by cutting and pasting the data from the within-subjects file.
4. Save the new file under a new name.

condition	recall
1.00	12.00
1.00	9.00
1.00	13.00
1.00	7.00
1.00	9.00
1.00	14.00
1.00	5.00
1.00	8.00
1.00	5.00
1.00	10.00
1.00	11.00
1.00	13.00
1.00	12.00
1.00	13.00
1.00	6.00
1.00	10.00
1.00	7.00
1.00	13.00
1.00	10.00
1.00	9.00

condition	recall
2.00	12.00
2.00	8.00
2.00	14.00
2.00	11.00
2.00	10.00
2.00	14.00
2.00	7.00
2.00	10.00
2.00	7.00
2.00	11.00
2.00	12.00
2.00	14.00
2.00	8.00
2.00	10.00
2.00	12.00
2.00	10.00
2.00	9.00
2.00	14.00
2.00	14.00
2.00	11.00

Because we are assuming there are different people in each group, we need to use an independent-samples *t*-test. Click

1. *Analyze*
2. *Compare means*
3. *Independent-samples t-test*
4. Move recall into the Test Variable box, and condition into the Grouping Variable box
5. Click *Define groups*
6. Enter a 1 for group 1 (our designation for the double letter condition) and 2 for group 2 (our designation for the concrete condition)
7. Click *Continue* and *OK*

Your output should look like this (again, the numbers will be different if you used your own data):

T-Test

		Group Statistics			
	condition	N	Mean	Std. Deviation	Std. Error Mean
recall	1.00	20	9.8000	2.82097	.63079
	2.00	20	10.9000	2.35975	.52766

Independent Samples Test

		Levene's Test for Equality of Variances		t-test for Equality of Means					95% Confidence Interval of the Difference	
		F	*Sig.*	*t*	*df*	*Sig. (2-tailed)*	*Mean Difference*	*Std. Error Difference*	*Lower*	*Upper*
recall	Equal variances assumed	.836	.366	−1.338	38	.189	−1.10000	.82238	−2.76483	.56483
	Equal variances not assumed			−1.338	36.850	.189	−1.10000	.82238	−2.76654	.56654

What's different about the outcome using this design? The descriptives are the same, but the values for *t, p,* and degrees of freedom have changed. This time the difference using the canned data is not significant. Why is that the case?

_____

_____

Bonus information: Notice that there are two rows containing information about *t, p,* and degrees of freedom. In this case they are very similar—only the values for degrees of freedom are different. How do you know which line to use? Look at the significance column for the Levene's Test for Equality of Variance. This statistic tests an underlying assumption of the independent *t*-test, equality of variance. If Levene's is significant, then the variances are significantly different, and therefore they are not equal. In that case use the line labeled "equal variances not assumed." If Levene's is not significant, then the variances are not significantly different, and can therefore be assumed to be equivalent. In that case use the line labeled "equal variances assumed."

Results

Data from the 20 participants were analyzed using a paired-samples *t*-test. Recall in the concrete condition (*M* = 10.0, *SD* = 2.36) was not significantly different from recall in the double letter condition (*M* = 9.8, *SD* = 2.82), *t*(38) = 1.34, *p* = .189. Contrary to the hypothesis, deeper encoding did not produce greater recall.

Several points for you to think about:

What was the purpose of this study? We wanted to test the Levels of Processing prediction that words more deeply encoded will be better recalled.

What did we hypothesize? Words processed for meaning (deeper processing) will be better recalled than those processed for spelling (shallow processing)—Double letter < Concrete

Why were you asked to think about something else (counting backwards by 3s) before you recalled the words? This is called a buffer-clearing task. When you have been attending to something, traces of it remain in your short-term memory for about 20–30 seconds. I wanted to get your mind off the words long enough for the words to decay from short-term memory. In other words, I wanted to know what you encoded in long-term memory and not what was still active in short-term memory.

Writing the Method Section

The method section is something like a recipe. It tells you exactly what was done, how it was done, and describes the participants. It should be so detailed that someone else could duplicate your experiment. This allows your reader to decide if you carried out your experiment appropriately. It would be hard to take experimental results seriously if the methods were sloppy or your measures unreliable or invalid. Give lots of details. Use the pointers from the "Closure" section of this lab to help you write a method section for this exercise.

Flexible Design

The two-group design can also be used to analyze data that don't qualify as a "true" experiment because assignment to groups wasn't random. For instance, if I had wanted to compare recall in males and females I couldn't randomly assign participants to the "male" or "female" group. When this happens you are using some characteristic of your participants as your IV, and this is called an ex post facto design. Despite the fact that it would not be a true experiment, I could still use the two-group design and the same types of analyses described above to compare the group means.

What if I'm Comparing Counts Instead of Means?

Sometimes you may want to compare the counts from two groups instead of means. In other words, you are using nominal data instead of ordinal, interval, or ratio data. For instructions on how to analyze this type of design, see the description of a chi-square (χ^2) analysis in Appendix 3.

Closure

Use the information below as a reminder of what should be included in a method section. Check the *APA Publication Manual* (p. 113–115) to see how the different levels of headings are formatted.

Method

Participants

Tell the reader the characteristics of your sample, such as how many participated, socioeconomic status, age, gender, ethnicity, health status, preferred language, or anything else that might help your reader interpret the findings. How were the participants recruited or selected? If the group is not representative, why not?

Materials

Describe all materials used. Identify the manufacturer of any specialized equipment. Why was each measurement instrument chosen? Have your measures been validated? Give an even more detailed description if you are using unpublished instruments.

Procedure

This is a step-by-step description of what occurred as you carried out the experiment and how you did it. What happened first? Then what? How were participants assigned to groups? How did you obtain informed consent? How did you ensure participants' confidentiality?

Three-Group Designs

Clinical Neuropsychology

DR. GEORGE DEMAKIS

Clinical neuropsychology is the assessment, treatment, and rehabilitation of individuals with known or suspected brain dysfunction, such as dementia, head injury, stroke, and learning disabilities. Assessment is a main focus in this area and neuropsychologists typically evaluate cognitive ability, such as attention, language, memory, and problem-solving, as well as emotional and personality functioning. As in many areas of psychology, the ability of neuropsychologists to perform the above tasks accurately is enhanced by research. Research in this area is, not surprisingly, quite broad and includes various types of designs, including case studies, correlational studies, and actual experiments. Case studies have been done on individuals with rare neurological disorders or unique presentations of common disorders. Correlational studies have examined the relationships between various neuropsychological tests in patients with specific disorders, such as Alzheimer's Disease. Experiments have been conducted on how various neurological surgeries, such as tumor removal, affect cognitive functioning.

Recently, there have been several areas of increased research emphasis including the following: cognitive outcomes after mild brain injury, the effect of chronic illicit drug use on cognitive performance, detection of poor effort or malingering on neuropsychological tests, and the relationship of performance on neuropsychological tests to activities of daily living.

Note to Instructor: You may wish to have students complete the lab on writing a Discussion section before completing the assignment below.

Assignment

The purpose of today's lab is to analyze data to demonstrate a three-group (one IV, 3 levels) experiment and write a complete lab report. Your write-up should include: (1) a title page, (2) an abstract, (3) an introduction, (4) a method section, (5) a results section, (6) a discussion section, and (7) a reference page. The paper should be in APA format. In order to do an introduction section you may need to do a little background reading on the topic, so you will need to find one or more relevant, peer-reviewed articles or a section of a textbook to help you bone up on the subject.

Topic

The effects of traumatic brain injury on IQ and memory in children.

Target Article

Campbell, C. G., Kuehn, S. M., Richards, P. M., Ventureyra, E., & Hutchinson, J. S. (2004). Medical and cognitive outcome in children with traumatic brain injury. *Canadian Journal of Neurological Science, 31*(2), 213–219.

Traumatic brain injury (TBI) can result from a concussion, or closed head injury. A mild injury may produce a brief change in consciousness, whereas a severe injury can result in a period of unconsciousness of 30 minutes or more. The injury may be associated with amnesia, impaired cognitive functioning, and may produce long-term disabilities or death. The article by Campbell et al. (2004) followed children aged 1 to 18 who had a moderate or severe head injury, measuring their cognitive and memory performance at three points in time: baseline (less than 4 months since the injury), early in the recovery process (5 to 15 months post injury), and during a follow-up period (16 to 38 months after injury). IQ scores moved from "low average" at baseline to average later in recovery, but a higher proportion of the scores remained more than 1.5 standard deviations below the mean than would be found in non-injured groups. Children who experienced a more severe coma were more likely to have lower IQ and verbal memory scores.

 For more information on traumatic brain injury from the Centers for Disease Control, go to http://www.cdc.gov/node.do/id/0900f3ec8000dbdc.

Our Study

Below are hypothetical data that you will analyze in two ways. There is one IV (time after injury) with three levels (baseline, early recovery, and follow-up).

Because you will analyze these data in two different ways, you will need to set up two different data files; however, you can use the cut and paste features to make this easy.

Between Subjects Design

First analyze the data as if it involved three groups of different individuals: one group that has a very recent TBI, one group that is recovering, and another group that has recovered from the injury and is being seen in follow-up. Since this is a between-subject design, you'll need one column to identify the IV (group membership; 1=baseline, 2=recovery, 3=follow-up) and a column for the DV (IQ scores). Enter the data, labeling the variables and identify the values for groups 1, 2, and 3.

aftr_tbi	IQ
1	86
1	95
1	90
1	88
1	87
1	65
1	67
1	70
1	71
1	84
2	91
2	100
2	95
2	89
2	93
2	85
2	87
2	82
2	88
2	96
3	101
3	102
3	99
3	92
3	104
3	88
3	95
3	93
3	99
3	105

Since you have more than two groups, you can't initially analyze the data using a series of *t* tests because of problems with family-wise error. You'll use a One-way Analysis of Variance (ANOVA).

SPSS instructions:

1. *Analyze*
2. *Compare means*
3. *One-way ANOVA*
4. Move the IQ score to the "Dependent" box and "aftr_tbi" to the "Factor" box.
5. We'll discuss options for post hoc tests later, but for now click *Post hoc, Tukey, Continue*
6. We'll compare the means for the three groups, so click *Options*
7. *Descriptive*
8. *Continue*
9. then *OK*

Descriptive

					95% Confidence Interval for Mean			
	N	Mean	Std. Deviation	Std. Error	Lower Bound	Upper Bound	Minimum	Maximum
baseline	10	80.3000	10.87352	3.43851	72.5216	88.0784	65.00	95.00
recovery	10	90.6000	5.48128	1.73333	86.6789	94.5211	82.00	100.00
followup	10	97.8000	5.59365	1.76887	93.7985	101.8015	88.00	105.00
Total	30	89.5667	10.44421	1.90684	58.6667	93.4666	65.00	105.00

Full IQ score

ANOVA

Full IQ score

	Sum of Squares	df	Mean Square	F	Sig.
Between Groups	1547.267	2	773.633	12.925	.000
Within Groups	1616.100	27	59.856		
Total	3163.367	29			

What did you find? Was the *F* test significant? Notice that *F* scores are reported with two values for degrees of freedom: the *df* associated with the effect you are reporting and the *df* for the error term. This would be reported using the following format: $F(2,27) = 12.92$, $p < .001$.

Note the placement of the degrees of freedom, the value of the *F* test, and the *p* value. Which letters should be italicized? _____

Since the *F* is significant you know that there is <u>at least</u> one significant difference among the three means, but you don't know specifically which means are significantly different. To find that out you must do some sort of post hoc ("after this") test. One option would be to do a series of three independent *t* tests. Another option is to use one of the post hoc tests provided by SPSS. You used the Tukey test this time.

Multiple Comparisons

Dependent Variable: Full IQ score

Tukey HSD

(I) Time after TBI	(J) Time after TBI	Mean Difference (I–J)	Std. Error	Sig.	95% Confidence Interval Lower Bound	Upper Bound
baseline	recovery	−10.3000*	3.45993	.016	−18.8786	−1.7214
	followup	−17.5000*	3.45993	.000	−26.0786	−8.9214
recovery	baseline	−10.3000*	3.45993	.016	1.7214	18.8786
	followup	−7.2000	3.45993	.113	−15.7786	1.3786
followup	baseline	17.5000*	3.45993	.000	8.9214	26.0786
	recovery	7.2000	3.45993	.113	−1.3786	15.7786

*The mean difference is significant at the .05 level.

What does the Tukey test tell you about the three possible comparisons (baseline compared to recovery, baseline compared to follow-up, and recovery compared to follow-up)? Which comparisons are significantly different? _____

Within Subjects Design

Now let's pretend that instead of comparing IQ scores for three <u>different</u> groups of children you followed the <u>same</u> children and measured each child's IQ at three different times after the TBI occurred. We'll use the same data, but this time we don't need a separate column to indicate group membership. Why not? _____

Since everyone has three IQ scores we'll need three columns of data, one for each level of the IV (i.e., test time). You can use the data you've already typed by deleting the "aftr_tbi" column, then cutting and pasting the recovery and follow-up scores into new columns. Label the columns.

baseline	recovery	followup
86.00	91.00	101.00
95.00	100.00	102.00
90.00	95.00	99.00
88.00	89.00	92.00

baseline	recovery	followup
87.00	93.00	104.00
65.00	85.00	88.00
67.00	87.00	95.00
70.00	82.00	93.00
71.00	88.00	99.00
84.00	96.00	105.00

Because you are measuring something in the same people "repeatedly" you'll need to use a "repeated measures" ANOVA.

1. Click *Analyze*
2. *General linear model*
3. *Repeated measures*
4. Now you are asked for a within-subject factor name. This is the IV—the time after the TBI when IQ was measured. Name the within-subject factor "testtime," indicate it has 3 levels, then
5. Click *Add*
6. *Define*
7. Highlight the three levels of the IV and move them into the "Within-subjects Variables" box. Ignore the other boxes for now.
8. Click *Options*
9. *Descriptive statistics*
10. *Continue*
11. *OK*

Your source table should look like this:

Tests of Within-Subject Effects

		Type III Sum of Squares	df	Mean Square	F	Sig.
Measure: MEASURE_1						
TESTTIME	Sphericity Assumed	1547.267	2	773.633	34.237	.000
	Greenhouse-Geisser	1547.267	1.263	1225.115	34.237	.000
	Huynh-Feidt	1547.267	1.374	1126.224	34.237	.000
	Lower-bound	1547.267	1.000	1547.267	34.237	.000
Error (TESTTIME)	Sphericity Assumed	406.733	18	22.596		
	Greenhouse-Geisser	406.733	11.367	35.783		
	Huynh-Feidt	406.733	12.365	32.895		
	Lower-bound	406.733	9.000	45.193		

But Wait—That's Not All!

There's a new twist to this analysis. Look higher up in your output for a box labeled "Mauchley's Test of Sphericity."

Mauchley's Test of Sphericity[a]

Measure: MEASURE_1

Within Subjects Effect	Mauchley's W	Approx. Chi-Square	df	Sig.	Greenhouse Geisser	Huynh-Feldt	Lower-bound
					Epsilon[b]		
Time	4.16	7.009	2	.030	.631	.687	.500

Tests the null hypothesis that the error covariance matrix of the orthonormalized transformed dependent variables is proportional to an identity matrix.

[a] Design: Intercept Within Subjects Design: time

[b] May be used to adjust the degrees of freedom for the averaged tests of significance. Corrected tests are displayed in the Tests of Within-Subjects Effects table.

This analysis tests an underlying assumption of ANOVA. If sphericity cannot be assumed, then that calls into doubt the F score and degrees of freedom. If Mauchley's **is not** significant then we **can** assume sphericity. If Mauchley's **is** significant, then we **cannot** assume sphericity. Why do we care? The Mauchley's test determines which F and degrees of freedom we report (and, therefore, whether the outcome is significant). Look in the source table above (Tests of Within-Subjects Effects). If Mauchley's test is not significant then report the values associated with "Sphericity Assumed." In this case, however, Mauchley's is significant—look at the value in the column labeled "Sig.," the value is less than .05, telling us an underlying assumption is violated by these data. Therefore, we'll have to report one of the other options (Greenhouse-Geisser, Huynh-Feldt, or Lower-bound). This lowers the degrees of freedom, therefore making your conclusion about significance more conservative. Let's go with Greenhouse-Geisser. In this case the F score is the same for all the methods, but look at the degrees of freedom. Those associated with Greenhouse-Geisser are 1.263 and 11.367. When you report the F, therefore, use those numbers [$F(1.263, 11.367) = . . .$].

Is the IV significant? _____ Report the F score. _____
Why can't I say $p = .000$?_____

Why is the F score so much larger this time? Hint: compare the "Mean Square Within Group" in the One-way ANOVA to the "Mean Square Error" in this ANOVA. Both of these terms refer to an estimate of error. _____

You still don't know which pairs of means are significantly different so you'll need to run post hoc tests. This time do a series of three paired-samples t tests. Why use paired tests instead of independent tests?

_____

What did you find? Report the means, standard deviations, t and p values for each pair.

		Paired Samples Test							
				Paired Differences					
					95% Confidence Interval of the Diffrence				Sig.
		Mean	Std. Deviation	Std. Error Mean	Lower	Upper	t	df	(2-tailed)
Pair 1	Full IQ score taken at baseline – Full IQ score taken during recovery	−10.3000	6.89686	2.18098	−15.2337	−5.3663	−4.723	9	.001
Pair 2	Full IQ score taken during recovery – Full IQ score taken during followup	−7.2000	3.76534	1.19070	−9.8936	−4.5064	−6.047	9	.000
Pair 3	Full IQ score taken at baseline – Full IQ score taken during followup	−17.5000	8.59263	2.71723	−23.6468	−11.3532	−6.440	9	.000

Test times compared   Statistics
Baseline vs. recovery $t(\_\_)=$_____, $p =$ _____
Recovery vs. follow-up $t(\_\_)=$_____, $p<$_____
Baseline vs. follow-up $t(\_\_)=$_____, $p<$_____

Describe the similarities and differences in the results of the two designs (between subjects vs. within subjects). What might explain the differences?

_____

_____

_____

_____

_____

_____

_____

Results

Choose the results of one of the designs used today and write a brief results section. Remember to tell the reader how you analyzed the data, state the findings (including means and standard deviations), and back it up with appropriate statistics. Report on the ANOVA first, then report any post hoc tests. When you are done, compare your results section to the sample below. Did you include all the important components? Did you report the statistics accurately, using good APA style?

_____

_____
_____
_____
_____
_____
_____
_____

The following example of a results section is specific to the repeated-measures design.

Results

A repeated-measures ANOVA tested for differences in IQ scores at the three test times after the injury. This produced a significant effect of test time, $F(1.263,11.367) = 34.24$, $p < .001$. Post hoc paired t-tests indicated that IQ scores increased from baseline ($M = 80.30$, $SD = 10.87$) to recovery ($M = 90.60$, $SD = 5.48$), $t(9) = 4.72$, $p = .001$ and from recovery to follow-up ($M = 97.80$, $SD = 5.59$), $t(9) = 6.05$, $p < .001$. The change from baseline to follow-up was also significant, $t(9) = 6.44$, $p < .001$.

Still Flexible

As was true for the two-group design, the three-group design can be used to analyze data that compare three group means even if it was not possible to randomly assign participants to the three groups. For example, if you had wanted to compare IQ among three groups of children—one group that had never had a brain injury, a group that had a brain injury prior to the age of 2, and a group whose brain injury occurred after the age of 2—you couldn't decide who went in each group—they came to you already in one of those groups. In this case we aren't doing a true experiment, but we're still doing a three-group comparison, and would analyze the data in the same way. Because it wouldn't be a true experiment, you'd have to be very cautious as to how you interpreted your findings.

Putting It All Together

Now it is time to integrate all that you've been learning about writing lab reports. You've practiced writing each section individually, so you are ready to write the entire lab report, all the way from title page to reference page. APA-style papers are double spaced throughout (even the references) and have a 1″ margin on all sides.

Collecting Your Own Data

If your instructor would like you to collect your own data, it probably will not be practical for you to track down and test people who have experienced a traumatic brain injury, nor have most of you been trained to administer, score and interpret the kinds of tests used by a clinical neuropsychologist. Therefore, I'm going to suggest a simpler but unrelated project that will let you practice using the three-group design. If you have a large class you can collect data from just yourselves. If you have a small class or would like to include a more representative sample you can collect information from others. Discuss with your instructor who your participants might be and how they will be recruited.

The Question

Let's see if there's a difference in the daytime sleepiness levels of three groups of people: those who report several characteristics of Internet addiction, those who report few symptoms, and those who report no symptoms. Let's hypothesize that people who show the most symptoms of Internet addiction will have greater daytime sleepiness (perhaps due to spending time on the Internet instead of sleeping). You can do background research on addictions in general and their association with sleep. An article you can use as a reference is

Nalwa, K. & Anand, A. P. (2003). Internet addiction in students: A cause of concern. *CyberPsychology and Behavior, 6*(6), 653–656.

The Instruments

Let's measure the extent of, or tendency toward, Internet addiction by developing a survey based on information found at http://addictionrecov. org/intwhat.htm. For each symptom of Internet addiction listed on this Web site, ask participants to indicate if that symptom is often true for them (2 points), sometimes true for them (1 point), or never true for them (0 points). For example, you might ask . . .

For each statement listed below indicate whether it is often true, sometimes true, or never true for you.

Do you stay on-line longer than originally intended?

_____ Never true

_____ Sometimes true

_____ Often true

These questions can be asked either in the form of a written survey, or by interviewing participants. In a small sample you may not identify anyone who would be diagnosed with an Internet addiction. Therefore, we'll simply compare lower and higher scores. Add up each person's points. First select the participants whose score was 1 or greater, then split the sample by doing a median split (those who had higher scores and those who had the lower scores). Identify each participant as being in one of three groups: those who answered "never true" to each symptom (total points = 0), those who answered "sometimes" or "often true" but had a lower total score, and those who had the highest scores.

Measure daytime sleepiness by using the Epsworth Sleepiness Scale which can be found, among other places, at http://www.stanford.edu/~dement/ epworth.html. Use the suggested scoring system and come up with a sleepiness score by totaling the points.

Now . . . follow the instructions given with the canned data above to compare the sleepiness scores of your three groups.

Cautions!

Make sure you come up with a system to guarantee anonymity or confidentiality. You are asking for sensitive information from your participants. Protect their privacy.

When asking about addictive behavior you may cause concern among your participants about whether or not they are experiencing addictive behavior. You aren't qualified to address this issue—neither am I—but there may be a counseling center on your campus that can be a resource for students. End the survey by suggesting that if the participant has any concerns about their Internet use they can seek assistance at the counseling center (or the student health center, or whatever resource is most appropriate).

Closure

More help with One-way ANOVAs:

http://www.wadsworth.com/psychology_d/templates/student_resources/ workshops/stat_workshp/one_anova/one_anova_01.html

Learn to graph your results—see the "Graphing" section in Appendix 4.

Factorial Designs

Clinical Psychology

DR. RICH TEDESCHI

Clinical psychologists have been busy for many years attempting to establish the degree to which psychotherapy produces improvement for persons with a variety of disorders. In 1995, the Task Force on Promotion and Dissemination of Psychological Procedures recommended that randomized clinical trials (RCTs), in which people are assigned to a treatment being studied and a comparison condition in a random fashion, are the best method for determining the efficacy of psychotherapy. This is an extension of the general experimental method to clinical questions.

In a clinical setting, this is actually a difficult kind of study to conduct. It is impossible to administer exactly the same treatment to each person, since people have somewhat different manifestations of problems, and therefore what is done in psychotherapy will vary to some extent. Researchers try to control this with the training of therapists through manuals that indicate how specifically to perform a psychotherapy under study, and then review recordings of these therapies to see that this was done. Another problem is random assignment of participants to groups—psychotherapy versus a comparison. Usually an initial screening must be done to assure that those assigned to both groups are close to equivalent on certain important aspects of diagnosis or other significant matters. It is also hard to set up the comparison group. Various approaches have been to use wait lists, no-treatment, or alternative treatments. Sometimes the "dismantling" approach is used where psychotherapy is given in its most complete form, compared with a form that leaves out what is thought to be a crucial aspect of it, in order to determine the effect of that aspect.

Finally, many clinical psychologists have argued that the most important elements of the psychotherapy effect have little to do with the specifics of the therapy approach, and more to do with characteristics of the therapist, the client, and especially, the relationship between the therapist and the client. Therefore, research has also been focused on measuring qualities of the therapeutic relationship, the "common factors" inherent in all psychotherapy treatments.

Assignment

Today you will analyze canned data from a 2×2 factorial design. You will analyze the same data in three different ways: once as if it were a completely within-subjects design, once as if it were a completely between-subjects design, and once as if it were a mixed factorial design. After that you'll write a complete lab report on the findings based on the mixed factorial design analysis—everything from the title and abstract to the reference page and table. This lab is a lot wordier than the others because factorial designs are more complex, and require a lot more explanation. Read it all, stick with me, and we'll get you through it. Turn in: complete lab report as described in the last lab.

Topic

What links alcohol consumption and aggression? Is aggression really the effect of alcohol, or could it be linked to *expectations* about the effects of alcohol?

Target Article

Lang, A. R., Goeckner, D. J., Adesso, V. J., & Marlatt, G. A. (1975). Effects of alcohol on aggression in male social drinkers. *Journal of Abnormal Psychology, 84*(5), 508–518.

This article actually used a more complex design than we will attempt. They used a $2 \times 2 \times 2$ factorial design. [Quick review: how many IVs were there (_____), and how many levels of each IV (_____)? How many cells (group means) were produced (_____)?] For the sake of our discussion, and to keep things as simple as possible, let's focus on just two of those IVs. Half the participants (all of whom identified themselves as heavy drinkers) were told that they would be consuming alcohol (vodka and tonic), and the other half were told they were consuming just tonic water. Half of each of those two groups actually drank alcohol, half actually drank tonic water. The vodka was sufficiently watered down so that the drinks tasted alike. Everyone was given enough liquid to produce—if alcohol was actually present—a blood alcohol level of .10. Aggression was measured as the duration and intensity of shocks the participant delivered to a confederate "learner," when the learner made an error. The variable not included in our discussion involved whether or not the participant was provoked to act aggressively. The authors found that the level of aggression had more to do with whether the participant thought he had consumed alcohol rather than whether he had actually consumed alcohol. In other words, his expectations about the effects of alcohol influenced aggression more so than did the alcohol itself.

Our Experiment

Let's assume that we're going to look at the effects of expectations about alcohol and the consumption of enough alcohol to produce a blood alcohol level of .12 on aggression. In other words, if we introduce more alcohol to this scenario, will the presence of alcohol cause aggression more than will expectations about alcohol? Will there be an interaction between what people expect to drink and what they actually drink? For example, would the effect of expectation on aggression depend on whether the person was drinking tonic water or alcohol?

Completely Between-Subjects Factorial Design

First let's imagine doing this task as a completely between-subjects 2×2 factorial design. This means there are different people in each of the four cells. The first variable in the data below indicates which expectation was established for each participant (1 = expected alcohol, 2 = expected water), the second indicates what each participant actually drank (1 = drank alcohol, 2 = drank water). The third column is the outcome measure. This score represents the duration and severity of shocks administered. Higher numbers indicate greater quantity and intensity of shocks administered to the learner.

expect	drank	aggress
1.00	1.00	240.00
1.00	1.00	231.00
1.00	1.00	188.00
1.00	1.00	197.00
1.00	1.00	155.00
1.00	1.00	242.00
1.00	1.00	215.00
1.00	1.00	190.00
1.00	1.00	179.00

expect	drank	aggress
1.00	1.00	167.00
1.00	2.00	221.00
1.00	2.00	207.00
1.00	2.00	187.00
1.00	2.00	173.00
1.00	2.00	129.00
1.00	2.00	223.00
1.00	2.00	209.00
1.00	2.00	189.00
1.00	2.00	165.00
1.00	2.00	141.00
2.00	1.00	196.00
2.00	1.00	162.00
2.00	1.00	142.00
2.00	1.00	140.00
2.00	1.00	160.00
2.00	1.00	204.00
2.00	1.00	173.00
2.00	1.00	179.00
2.00	1.00	175.00
2.00	1.00	134.00
2.00	2.00	198.00
2.00	2.00	164.00
2.00	2.00	144.00
2.00	2.00	142.00
2.00	2.00	128.00
2.00	2.00	206.00
2.00	2.00	175.00
2.00	2.00	181.00
2.00	2.00	177.00
2.00	2.00	108.00

Remember to label your variables and indicate the meaning of the assigned values.

Because both IVs are between-subjects, we'll use the univariate ANOVA to analyze these data.

1. Click *Analyze*
2. *General linear model*
3. *Univariate*
4. Move the two IVs into the Fixed Factors box and the DV into the Dependent Variable box.
5. Go to *Options*, and click the box to the left of *Descriptives*.
6. Finish with *Continue*
7. *OK*

Univariate Analysis of Variance

Between-Subject Factors

		Value Label	N
expected to drink	1.00	alcohol	20
	2.00	water	20
actually drank	1.00	alcohol	20
	2.00	water	20

This box lets you make sure you set up the analysis correctly.

Descriptive Statistics

Dependent Variable: aggression level/intensity

expected to drink	actually drank	Mean	Std. Deviation	N
alcohol	alcohol	200.4000	30.47112	10
	water	184.4000	32.37351	10
	Total	192.4000	31.67998	20
water	alcohol	166.5000	23.49586	10
	water	162.3000	31.24473	10
	Total	164.4000	26.99201	20
Total	alcohol	183.4500	31.68176	20
	water	173.3500	32.97571	20
	Total	178.4000	32.32511	40

You'll need this information when you interpret your results.

Tests of Between-Subject Effects

Dependent Variable: aggression level/intensity

Source	Type III Sum of Squares	df	Mean Square	F	Sig.
Corrected Model	9208.200[a]	3	3069.400	3.503	.025
Intercept	1273062.400	1	1273062.400	1452.927	.000
expect	7840.000	1	7840.000	8.948	.005
drank	1020.100	1	1020.100	1.164	.288
expect × drank	348.100	1	348.100	.397	.532
Error	31543.400	36	876.206		
Total	1313814.000	40			
Corrected Total	40751.600	39			

[a]R Squared = .226 (Adjusted R Squared = .161)

Notice that this analysis gives you an *F* value for each main effect (each variable by itself, not taking into consideration the other variables), as well as an *F* value for the interaction effect of "expect × drank." You will now examine each main effect and the interaction effect to determine if any is significant, and indicate this below. Refer back to the previous lab for the format to use when reporting *F* scores. Notice which parts are italicized. Be sure you understand where each number is found in the source table.

Is the main effect of "expect" significant? _____ Report the *F* value and significance level. _____

Is the main effect of "drank" significant? _____ Report the *F* value and significance level. _____

Is the "expect × drank" interaction effect significant? _____ Report the *F* value and significance level. _____

As we indicated earlier, when there are <u>three or more</u> means involved in an effect, then it is necessary to do some type of post hoc test. Are post hoc tests needed to further test the significant main effect of "expect"? _____ Why? (Hint: How many means are being compared by the "expect" main effect?)

_____

So . . . using this design we can conclude that, like Lang et al. (1975), we found that *expecting* to drink alcohol produced more aggression than found when expecting to drink water. Here, what people *actually* drank didn't produce a difference in aggression, nor was there a significant interaction between people's expectations and what they actually drank.

Mixed-Factorial Design

Next let's treat the data as if they had been produced using a mixed factorial design. In a mixed factorial design there is at least one between-subjects IV and at least one within-subjects IV. Remember, one enters data differently for between- and within-subjects variables. In this case, let's assume that what people expected to drink was the between-subjects variable (different people) and what they actually drank was the within-subjects variable (same people tested twice, once drinking alcohol and once drinking water).

The order of drink presentation was counterbalanced. What does this mean?

_____

_____

We need one column to indicate the expectation condition and two columns to indicate the DV under two different drinking conditions (aggression when drinking alcohol, aggression when drinking water). Let 1 = expected to drink alcohol and 2 = expected to drink water.

expect	agg_d_a	agg_d_w
1.00	240.00	221.00
1.00	231.00	207.00
1.00	188.00	187.00
1.00	197.00	173.00
1.00	155.00	129.00
1.00	242.00	223.00
1.00	215.00	209.00
1.00	190.00	189.00
1.00	179.00	165.00
1.00	167.00	141.00
2.00	196.00	198.00
2.00	162.00	164.00
2.00	142.00	144.00
2.00	140.00	142.00
2.00	160.00	128.00
2.00	204.00	206.00
2.00	173.00	175.00
2.00	179.00	181.00
2.00	175.00	177.00
2.00	134.00	108.00

How many participants did we have for the completely between-subjects design? _____ How many do we have for the mixed-factorial design? _____ Why do we have fewer participants this time? _____

Since we now have a repeated-measure variable, we'll need to use the Repeated Measures ANOVA.

1. Click *Analyze*
2. *General linear model*
3. *Repeated measures*
4. What people actually drank is the repeated-measures variable, so make the within subject factor name "drank," indicate it has 2 levels, then click
5. *Add*
6. *Define*
7. Highlight the two aggression variable names and move them using the right arrow into the "within-subjects variable" box.
8. Move *Expect* to the *Between-subjects factor* box
9. Click *Options*
10. *Descriptive statistics*
11. *Continue*
12. *OK*

The output will contain more information than we're going to use just now, so I'll reproduce here only the information we'll use.

General Linear Model

Within-Subjects Factors

Measure: MEASURE_1

drank	Dependent Variable
1	agg_d_a
2	agg_d_w

Between-Subjects Factors

		Value Label	N
expected to drink	1.00	alcohol	10
	2.00	water	10

Use these boxes to make sure you set up the variables the way you intended to do.

Descriptive Statistics

	expected to drink	Mean	Std. Deviation	N
aggression when drinking alcohol	alcohol	200.4000	30.47112	10
	water	166.5000	23.49586	10
	Total	183.4500	31.68176	20
aggression when drinking water	alcohol	184.4000	32.37351	10
	water	162.3000	31.24473	10
	Total	173.3500	32.97571	20

By now you know how you'll use the descriptive information.

Tests of Within-Subjects Effects

Measure: MEASURE_1

Source		Type III Sum of Squares	df	Mean Square	F	Sig.
drank	Sphericity Assumed	1020.100	1	1020.100	14.955	.001
	Greenhouse-Geisser	1020.100	1.000	1020.100	14.955	.001
	Huynh-Feldt	1020.100	1.000	1020.100	14.955	.001
	Lower-bound	1020.100	1.000	1020.100	14.955	.001
drank × expect	Sphericity Assumed	348.100	1	348.100	5.103	.037
	Greenhouse-Geisser	348.100	1.000	348.100	5.103	.037
	Huynh-Feldt	348.100	1.000	348.100	5.103	.037
	Lower-bound	348.100	1.000	348.100	5.103	.037

(continued)

Tests of Within-Subjects Effects (continued)

Source		Type III Sum of Squares	df	Mean Square	F	Sig.
Error (drank)	Sphericity Assumed	1227.800	18	68.211		
	Greenhouse-Geisser	1227.800	18.000	68.211		
	Huynh-Feldt	1227.800	18.000	68.211		
	Lower-bound	1227.800	18.000	68.211		

For our purposes, use the values associated with "sphericity assumed." Now we get to some new stuff. This box reports the within-subjects main effect and any interactions involving a within-subjects variable. The box below reports the between-subjects main effects, and would also report interaction effects of between-subjects variables (we don't have any). Notice each box has its own error term and *df*.

Tests of Between-Subjects Effects

Measure: MEASURE_1					
Transformed Variable: Average					
Source	Type III Sum of Squares	df	Mean Square	F	Sig.
Intercept	1273062.400	1	1273062.400	755.886	.000
expect	7840.000	1	7840.000	4.655	.045
Error	30315.600	18	1684.200		

Is the main effect of "drank" significant? _____ Is the main effect of "expect" significant? _____ Is the "drank × expect" interaction effect significant? _____ Using a different design changed the outcome despite the fact that we used the same data.

A significant *F* means that somewhere among all the means involved in that effect there is at least one significant difference. If there are only two means, as is true for the main effects of "expect" and "drank," then you don't need to do post hoc tests. However, this time the interaction effect is significant, and it involves four means, so you'll have to do some sort of post hoc tests to find the significantly different means.

Here are the means in table form.

	Expected	
	Alcohol	Water
Drank Alcohol	200.4	166.5
Drank Water	180.4	162.3

There are different types of post hoc tests you can use. For now I'm going to illustrate *t*-tests. Remember, this is a mixed factorial design, so when you are comparing what people <u>expected to drink</u> (in each column), there are <u>different</u> people in each group and you must use the independent-samples *t*-test. When you are comparing the effects of what people <u>actually drank</u> (in each row) you are comparing the <u>same people</u> tested under two different conditions. For these comparisons use the paired-samples *t* test.

We need to make four comparisons.

Comparison # 1: Among those who expected to drink alcohol, did what people actually drink affect aggression levels? This compares 200.4 to 180.4. You want to narrow down your data to just those participants who expected to drink alcohol, so from the data screen click

1. *Data*
2. *Select cases*
3. *If condition is satisfied*
4. *If*
5. We coded "expected to drink alcohol" as 1. Highlight "expect," move it to the box on the right, then type in "=1."
6. Click *Continue*
7. *OK*

This takes you back to the data screen. You should see the participants who expected to drink water now have a slash over their subject number, indicating that they won't be included in your next test, and SPSS has created a "filter" variable. When we compare aggression when drinking alcohol to aggression when drinking water, we are comparing the same people, so run a paired *t* test. Is this comparison significant? _____ Write out this statistic and level of significance.

_____

Helpful hint: It is very easy to forget which group is included in a particular test when you have selected a subset of your participants. As soon as I ran this paired-samples *t* test, I went back up to the title "T Test" at the top of this output and clicked it. I then went up to the small button on the toolbar that lets you "insert note." It looks like a piece of paper with the top-right corner folded down with ^ underneath it. Type "people who expected to drink alcohol" in this box, so you will remember later which subgroup it represents.

Comparison #2: Now go back to the data screen and

1. have the computer select for "expect = 2," the people who expected to drink water. This compares 166.5 to 162.3.
2. Test these with the paired *t* test.
3. Insert a note to label this test, too. Is it significant? _____ Write it out. _____

Before we go any further, go back to the data screen,

1. Click *Data*
2. *Select cases*
3. *All cases*
4. *OK*

Now everyone is included again.

Comparisons 3 & 4: The next two comparisons examine the effects of expectation on aggression when drinking alcohol (comparison #3) and aggression when drinking water (comparison #4). These compare 200.4 to 166.5 and 180.4 to 162.3. These two comparisons involve <u>different</u> people in each group so you test them using the _____-samples *t*-test.

1. Use "expect" as the grouping variable (remember to define it).
2. Use "aggression when drinking alcohol" as the test variable.
3. Actually, you can run both *t* tests at one time. Go ahead and move the "aggression when drinking water" variable name to the test variable box as well. The computer will run a *t* test for each variable.

What did you find from these two comparisons?

_____

_____

_____

Thus far, then, we can conclude, using the mixed-factorial design, that . . .

✓ 200.4 > 180.4, $t(9) = 5.06$, $p = .001$ [people who expected to drink alcohol were more aggressive when they actually drank alcohol than when they actually drank water]

✓ 166.5 = 162.3, $t(9) = 1.01$, $p = .339$ [people who expected to drink water were equally aggressive regardless of what they actually drank]

✓ 200.4 > 166.5, $t(18) = 2.786$. $p = .012$ [when people actually drank alcohol, they showed more aggression if they had expected to drink alcohol than if they had expected to drink water]

✓ 184.4 = 162.3, $t(18) = 1.553$, $p = .138$ [when people actually drank water, they showed the same level of aggression regardless of whether they expected to drink alcohol or water]

Interpretation of the Mixed Factorial Design

Confused yet? Interactions can be a challenge to recognize and interpret. Let's try to sort it out.

The Research Questions

We had wondered whether using a higher blood alcohol level would produce a significant effect of what people actually drank, and whether participants' expectations would interact with what they actually drank.

What We Found and What It Indicates

We found significant main effects of both "expect" and "drank" as well as a significant interaction of the two variables. The main effects tell us that people are more aggressive when they think they are drinking alcohol and more aggressive when they actually drink alcohol. However, since we have the significant interaction effect, we have to say that those main effects are modified by the significant interaction. In other words, the main effects don't tell the whole story. The interaction tells us that although people who expected to drink alcohol were more aggressive when actually drinking alcohol, the main effect of what they drank was modified by what they expected to drink. In other words, the main effect of what people drank depended on their expectations. If they expected water, they were no more aggressive when drinking alcohol than water. Of all the participants who drank alcohol, alcohol's tendency to increase aggression was seen only when they also expected to drink alcohol. When drinking water, expectations had no impact on aggression.

The significant interaction tells us that we can't make a statement about the effects of expectations or the effects of what one actually drank without taking into consideration the other variable. Do you get the feeling that your Results section just got a lot longer?

Completely Within-Subjects Factorial Design

Let's do one more analysis. This time assume that each participant participated in each of the four possible conditions. This would be a completely within-subjects design. There is no between-subjects variable; rather, there are two within-subjects variables. This time, 10 participants are tested on four different occasions. The four variables below are:

ex_a_d_a	Expected alcohol, drank alcohol
ex_a_d_w	Expected alcohol, drank water
ex_w_d_a	Expected water, drank alcohol
ex_w_d_w	Expected water, drank water

ex_a_d_a	ex_a_d_w	ex_w_d_a	ex_w_d_w
240.00	221.00	196.00	198.00
231.00	207.00	162.00	164.00
188.00	187.00	142.00	144.00
197.00	173.00	140.00	142.00
155.00	129.00	160.00	128.00
242.00	223.00	204.00	206.00
215.00	209.00	173.00	175.00
190.00	189.00	179.00	181.00
179.00	165.00	175.00	177.00
167.00	141.00	134.00	108.00

1. Click *Analyze*
2. *General linear model*
3. *Repeated measures*
4. If there is already a variable name in the first large box, highlight it and click remove.
5. We must now set up two within-subjects variables. The first variable is expectation: the first two columns are aggression levels when alcohol was expected, the next two when water was expected.
6. So let's make the first variable "expect," indicate it has 2 levels, then add it to the large box.
7. Now, notice that within each level of expectation, the first column indicates the participants actually drank alcohol, and the next column indicates they drank water. The second within-subjects variable, therefore, is what people actually drank.
8. Let's call it "drank," indicate it has 2 levels
9. Then click *Add*
10. *Define*
11. Highlight the 4 variables and move them to the "within-subjects variables" box.
12. *Options*
13. *Descriptives*
14. *Continue*
15. *OK*

Again, I include here only the information that we'll use.

General Linear Model

Within-Subjects Factors		

Measure: MEASURE_1

expect	drank	Dependent Variable
1	1	ex_a_d_a
	2	ex_a_d_w
2	1	ex_w_d_a
	2	ex_w_d_w

Descriptive Statistics			
	Mean	Std. Deviation	N
expect alcohol, drank alcohol	200.4000	30.47112	10
expect alcohol, drank water	184.4000	32.37351	10
expect water, drank alcohol	166.5000	23.49586	10
expect water, drank water	162.3000	31.24473	10

Tests of Within-Subjects Effects

Source		Type III Sum of Squares	df	Mean Square	F	Sig.
		Measure: MEASURE_1				
expect	Sphericity Assumed	7840.000	1	7840.000	18.897	.002
	Greenhouse-Geisser	7840.000	1.000	7840.000	18.897	.002
	Huynh-Feldt	7840.000	1.000	7840.000	18.897	.002
	Lower-bound	7840.000	1.000	7840.000	18.897	.002
Error (expect)	Sphericity Assumed	3734.000	9	414.889		
	Greenhouse-Geisser	3734.000	9.000	414.889		
	Huynh-Feldt	3734.000	9.000	414.889		
	Lower-bound	3734.000	9.000	414.889		
drank	Sphericity Assumed	1020.100	1	1020.100	9.937	.012
	Greenhouse-Geisser	1020.100	1.000	1020.100	9.937	.012
	Huynh-Feldt	1020.100	1.000	1020.100	9.937	.012
	Lower-bound	1020.100	1.000	1020.100	9.937	.012
Error (drank)	Sphericity Assumed	923.900	9	102.656		
	Greenhouse-Geisser	923.900	9.000	102.656		
	Huynh-Feldt	923.900	9.000	102.656		
	Lower-bound	923.900	9.000	102.656		
expect × drank	Sphericity Assumed	348.100	1	348.100	10.309	.011
	Greenhouse-Geisser	348.100	1.000	348.100	10.309	.011
	Huynh-Feldt	348.100	1.000	348.100	10.309	.011
	Lower-bound	348.100	1.000	348.100	10.309	.011
Error (expect × drank)	Sphericity Assumed	303.900	9	33.767		
	Greenhouse-Geisser	303.900	9.000	33.767		
	Huynh-Feldt	303.900	9.000	33.767		
	Lower-bound	303.900	9.000	33.767		

Notice that this time each main effect and each interaction has its very own error term. Are the main effects significant? _____ Is the interaction significant? _____ Write out the F term and level of significance for each effect.

Main effect of "expect" _____

Main effect of "drank" _____

Interaction effect of "expect × drank" _____

The results are similar to those of the mixed factorial design, so we won't wade through all the post hoc tests this time. If we did, however, which t tests would you use for all four comparisons (remember—the same participants are in all four groups)? _____-samples t tests

Just to be sure you could do it if you needed to, list the pairs that you would test using these *t*-tests:

_____ compared to _____

_____ compared to _____

_____ compared to _____

_____ compared to _____

And now, at last (drumroll), the instruction part of this lab is done. In addition to running the analyses called for in this lab, your instructor may want you to write a complete lab report using the mixed-factorial data from this exercise. "Complete" means title page, abstract, introduction, method, results, discussion, references, and table. See page 315 of the *Publication Manual* for an illustration of a properly formatted table. Notice that the table comes on a separate page after the references. By now you know what goes in a results section, so you're on your own! Congratulations, you're now done with the most difficult and lengthy part of this lab manual!!

Collecting Your Own Data

If your instructor would like you to use this design to collect your own data, here is a suggestion. I recommend that you do not try anything more complex than a 2 × 2 factorial design. Either individually or as a group, come up with two IVs and a DV that can test the following experimental hypothesis.

You wonder whether men or women more strongly endorse appropriate sex-typed behavior in children, and whether those ideas differ depending on the gender of the child. You predict that men will generally endorse stereotypical behavior more strongly than women, and that their endorsement will be especially strong for boys.

Suggestions about Measures . . .

You could put together pictures or descriptions of children playing with non-stereotypical toys. For example, you might represent a boy playing in a toy kitchen or a girl playing with race cars. You could come up with some type of rating scale that indicates how men and women feel about girls and boys playing with toys generally associated with the other gender.

Some Suggestions about Methodology . . .

Control for potential confounds by making all the children about the same age. Have equal numbers of pictures/descriptions of boys and girls.

To Think about . . .

Will your design be completely between-subjects, completely within-subjects, or a mixed factorial design? Discuss this in advance and decide how you will analyze your data.

Decide on the variables, decide who the participants will be, how many you will need to recruit, and how you will recruit them, assemble the materials, then collect and analyze your data.

Closure

More Practice with Interactions

 Let's do some extra practice with interactions. Begin by reading http://www.wadsworth.com/psychology_d/templates/student_resources/workshops/stat_workshp/two_anova/two_anova_01.html.

Remember that when you have to say "it depends" to describe the effect of a variable on some outcome, then you probably have an interaction between two variables. In order to describe the effect of one variable you have to qualify it by noting the effect of another variable.

Identify each effect below as a main effect or an interaction effect. Remember, interaction effects tell you that the effect of one variable depends on the level of the other variable.

_____ 1. People with higher intelligence tend to have better physical health.

_____ 2. Older children generally use more effective memory strategies than do younger children.

_____ 3. Adults usually show better recall than children, but it depends on the participants' knowledge and the type of memory task. Children who are chess experts remember more chess positions than adults who are chess novices, although adults remember longer strings of unrelated numbers than do children.

_____ 4. Female college students expect the instructor to consider effort when assigning a grade more than do male college students.

_____ 5. Medication improved depression levels, but only when it was combined with therapy.

There are two interaction effects listed above.* How did you know they were interactions?

_____

_____

_____

*Statements 3 and 5 describe interaction effects.

_____

_____

You conduct a 2 × 2 factorial experiment examining the effects of age (young adult, older adult) and health (good health, poor health) on memory. You have a significant main effect of age and a significant interaction of age and health. What does this mean?

_____

_____

Identify the two IVs and one DV.

IVs: _____   _____

DV: _____

Let's assume these are your means (higher numbers indicate greater recall):

Health		
	Poor	Good
Younger	16.41	18.90
Older	11.57	18.62

If the <u>main effect</u> of Health is significant, will you need to do post hoc tests? _____ If the <u>interaction effect</u> of Age × Health is significant, will you need to do post hoc tests? _____ Assume a completely between-subjects design was used. For the Health variable, let 1 = poor health and 2 = good health. For the Age variable, let 1 = younger and 2 = older. If you need to do the post hoc tests for this interaction, what must you do?

Select if Health = ___, then do a(n) _____-samples t-test comparing _____

Select if Health = ___, then do a(n) _____-samples t-test comparing _____

Select if Age = ___, then do a(n) _____-samples t-test comparing _____

Select if Age = ___, then do a(n) _____-samples t-test comparing _____

Single Subject Designs

Behavior Analysis

DR. PETE LAMAL

Behavior analysis is the study of what humans and nonhumans do, including language (verbal behavior). The emphasis is on the role of the environment, while not denying the importance of hereditary factors. The areas of behavior analysis are basic, applied, and conceptual. Basic behavior analysis is the study of humans and nonhumans, usually in the laboratory under controlled (i.e. experimental) conditions. The emphasis is on the study of individuals rather than groups. Applied behavior analysis is the study of humans and nonhumans, usually outside the laboratory, in attempts to improve their ability to function more adequately. The conceptual area is concerned with the consideration of the philosophical underpinnings of behavior analysis, particularly as to how they differ from the conceptual bases of other viewpoints.

Basic behavior analysis is credited with establishing such principles as positive reinforcement, schedules of reinforcement, and stimulus control. Applied behavior analysis is widely used in the treatment of individuals with autism, in education, in business and industry, and parenting. Conceptual behavior analysis has clarified the similarities and differences between behavior analysis and other viewpoints, e.g., cognitive psychology.

Assignment

Behavior modification can be used by a therapist to help a client change behavior. In this lab you will serve as your own participant. You are going to use behavior modification on yourself to change some behavior. Is there a bad habit you'd like to stop or a good one you'd like to begin or increase? Here's your chance! The end product of this lab will be a poster describing your project and the results. Your instructor will give you the details regarding length. This lab will take a few weeks, so you may need to start it early. As in earlier labs, I'll provide canned data, in case it is not possible or feasible to collect your own data. Turn in: poster describing a study in which you attempt to modify your own behavior.

Topic

Behavior Modification—Would You Like Ketchup With That?

Target Article

Ahearn, W. H. (2003). Using simultaneous presentation to increase vegetables consumption in a mildly selective child with autism. *Journal of Applied Behavior Analysis, 36*(3), 361–365.

This single case study is of a teenage boy with autism and mental retardation who would not eat vegetables. The experimenter paired presentation of vegetables with the presence of condiments such as ketchup, mustard, and salad dressing. The design used was ABABAB, in which A was baseline (no condiments) and B was the experimental phase (condiments present). The child ate more vegetables when they came with condiments.

It's All about You

Follow these instructions to conduct a self-modification study for one week. Note that you will report data using an ABA (baseline, intervention, return to baseline) design. The intervention (part B) should last at least one full week. After you have observed your own behavior, you will put together an oral presentation or a poster to describe your results. You will be "eyeballing" the data rather than running a statistical test. Compare the frequency of the targeted behavior from the first baseline days, the intervention days, and the second baseline days. Put your results into a graph or table. In order to provide some background information, you may need to do a little reading on the topic, so you may need to find a relevant article or a section of a textbook to help you bone up on the subject.

Procedure

Pick a behavior you want to change. It can involve either beginning or increasing a desired behavior or ending or decreasing an undesired behavior.

Be very specific. Choose something that is observable and measurable. For example, "improving my health" is vague; "decreasing the number of cigarettes smoked per day" is specific.

Decide on your motivation. If you want to increase a behavior, think of a meaningful way to reward yourself. If you want to decrease a behavior, think of a punishment (for example, denying yourself TV time or keeping a rubber band on your wrist and "snapping" yourself every time you commit the undesired behavior).

A. Measure the behavior at baseline. Before you begin your reward/punishment program, measure the behavior for at least three days. Record this information.
B. Begin your intervention. For one week, keep track of how many times the target behavior occurs. Make use of your reward/punishment every time you repeat the behavior. Record this information daily.
C. Return to baseline. After a week of intervention, stop rewarding or punishing yourself and record the occurrence of the behavior for another three days. Does it return to the pre-intervention level or stay changed?

Canned Data

Let's pretend that you wanted to increase the number of minutes spent studying. You measure your baseline study time for three days, then for one week you give yourself five minutes of video game time for every 30 minutes you spend studying. After a week you suspend the video reward but continue to measure your study time. Here are your findings.

	Total minutes spent studying
Baseline day 1	45
Baseline day 2	37
Baseline day 3	23
Intervention day 1	30
Intervention day 2	35
Intervention day 3	45
Intervention day 4	60
Intervention day 5	50
Intervention day 6	73
Intervention day 7	59
Back to baseline day 1	52
Back to baseline day 2	61
Back to baseline day 3	64

What is the average for the first baseline period? _____

What is the average for the intervention period? _____

What is the average for the return to baseline period? _____

When Would I Use a Poster?

Professional conferences almost always attract more people who want to present their research than can be accommodated. Rather than giving an oral presentation, many researchers opt for a poster presentation. Many more poster presentations can be accepted than oral presentations. A poster is a great way to begin presenting at conferences.

Ask your instructor about any undergraduate research conferences in your area, then make arrangements to present a poster there. In addition, consider getting a student membership to the relevant professional organization(s) and attending their conferences. Your instructor can help you identify the professional organizations related to your areas of interest.

What Happens during a Poster Presentation?

Once your poster has been accepted for presentation at a conference you will be notified of the time and place it is to be displayed, as well as any information on preparing your poster. Poster presentations are often done in large ballrooms that can accommodate many posters at one time. Interested people will have seen the abstract or title of your poster in the program book and will plan to come by and look at it. At your assigned time you hang your poster in the designated spot, and wait for people to come by to discuss your research with you. Plan to stay with your poster throughout the session. Be prepared to answer questions about your project, listen to new interpretations of your findings, meet other researchers with your same interests, network, hobnob, and generally have a good time talking about research. It is a good idea to bring copies of a handout describing your poster so interested people can take a copy with them.

What Information Goes on the Poster?

The same elements of a manuscript are used on a poster, but they are very brief. You generally use some type of banner or title board to indicate the title of your study, your name and organization. You will give a very brief introduction, a bare-bones description of your methods, your results, and conclusions. The length of each section will be determined by available space. At many conferences, posters must be no larger than 8′ × 4′. Your instructor will give you more specific details about your poster.

How Should the Poster Be Organized?

Remember that posters are intended to be read as people walk by. Your poster, therefore, must be in **large type** so it can be read from a distance of about 4–8 feet. One fourth of an inch might be the minimum size. I prefer to use a sans serif font such as Arial. Headings are slightly larger than the text. You have a limited amount of space, so every word, figure, or table must be necessary and concise. Since people will be reading as they walk, organize your information from left to right so it can be read with one pass. For example, you might arrange your poster like the figure below. Each rectangle represents a piece of paper.

| Title of My Poster
Your name, along with any coauthors
Name of your university | | | |

Abstract Summarize your study in one paragraph . . . 1	. . . finish introduction, state purpose and hypothesis of your study . . . 4	Results Describe most important findings . . . you may wish to list them as bullets . . . 7	Discussion Very briefly state what you think are the most important findings and what they may indicate . . . 10
Title Begin introduction . . . 2	Method Very briefly describe participants, materials, procedure 5	. . . more results . . . . . . insert tables or figures to illustruate points as needed . . . 8	. . . more discussion . . . 11
. . . continue introduction . . . 3	. . . continue method . . . 6	. . . more results, figures, tables . . . 9	References The most relevant references to your study 12

Closure

For further information about self-modification programs, consult one of the books listed below or a similar book.

Weiten, W., & Lloyd, M. A. (2000). *Psychology applied to modern life: Adjustment at the turn of the century* (6th ed.). Belmont, CA: Wadsworth.

Watson, D. L., & Tharp, R. G. (1993). *Self-directed behavior: Self-modification for personal adjustment* (6th ed.). Pacific Grove, CA: Brooks/Cole.

 For a quick review of the terminology and principles of behavior modification, see http://chiron.valdosta.edu/whuitt/col/behsys/behmod.html.

Who Uses Behavior Modification?

Behavior modification has been used to change children's behavior, although at times a parent will tell you it usually works better with other people's children. It has been used to deal with unnecessary crying at night by infants, potty training in toddlers, children with behavioral disorders, troubled teenagers, and so on. And we all know that children can be very successful at modifying the behavior of their parents! Of course, behavior modification isn't limited to humans. It is also used to train pets and working or performing animals.

Are you interested in methods for treating eating disorders? There is an issue of the journal *Behavior Modification* that is devoted to that topic. See volume *26*(6), 2004.

Part IV

Designing and Reporting Your Study

Designing Your Study

Cognition and Aging

DR. PAUL FOOS

A common belief for hundreds of years has been that our memories and higher cognitive functions like decision-making, problem-solving, and creativity decline as we grow older. More recently, researchers have been able to examine these proposed changes in cognition, while controlling a number of extraneous variables. We now know that some changes do occur in memory. Older adults have fewer resources available to process incoming and important information and take longer to retrieve episodic memories. On the positive side, older adults are generally quite good at retrieving semantic memories and are far more likely to show wisdom than younger adults.

Two extraneous variables that researchers have had to control in order to arrive at valid conclusions about changes in adult memory are distractions and slowing. We know that older adults are more easily distracted while performing a task. This seems to be due to the breakdown of inhibitory systems in the brain, and if one is not careful when comparing old and young, one might conclude a processing difference when in fact the task was performed under distracting conditions. Older adults (as well as young adults) perform better when distractions are minimized. Older adults also process information more slowly than younger adults. It may not be that older adults cannot perform some tasks as well; it may simply be that they take longer to do so. Given sufficient time, they perform at the same level as younger adults.

Assignment

The purpose of this lab is to help you take the information you've learned on the topic you chose for your literature review and use it to develop a research question or hypothesis, and begin to plan the design and details of your project. Turn in: a description of a new study that arises from one previously published (four short-answer questions below), and the structure of the study you will conduct.

Topic

The effects of cardiovascular and metabolic disease on cognition among older adults

Target Article

Verhaeghen, P., Borchelt, M., & Smith, J. (2003). Relation between cardiovascular and metabolic disease and cognition in very old age: Cross-sectional and longitudinal findings from the Berlin Aging Study. *Health Psychology, 22*(6), 559–569.

As people age some aspects of cognition may decline as may their physical health. Since both aging and some diseases might impair cognition, it is useful to design a study that looks at the effects of these two processes separately. Verhaeghen et al. (2003) studied cognition, cardiovascular disease, and diabetes in older adults (age 70 and up). They studied their participants both cross-sectionally (comparing older adults with or without one of these diseases) and longitudinally (changes in cognition over time in the same adults). They found that both diseases were associated with impaired cognition over and above the effects of age, socioeconomic status, and dementia.

 See http://www.cdc.gov/health/cardiov.htm for more information about cardiovascular disease and http://www.cdc.gov/health/diabetes.htm for more information about diabetes.

Using Existing Research as a Springboard for Future Research

Your task today will be to practice using one study as a tool for developing a new research question. You've now completed your literature review and have some knowledge about your topic. Now it is time to build on that knowledge and propose a research question for your own project.

First, let's think about ways in which new research projects can be developed from previous studies.

1. An article may suggest a useful follow-up study in its discussion section. There's no reason you can't follow up on that suggestion (giving appropriate credit, of course, to the original author)!
2. You may find that some of your articles produced results consistent with one interpretation or theory, while others indicated something different. You can design a study that tries to resolve the discrepancies.
3. What questions about this topic still have not been investigated? If you notice a "hole" in the literature you can design a study to address that issue. For example, in the study cited here you might think that the next logical step is to see if successful management of a disease produces improvements in cognition.
4. Is there a way to apply the findings from a study? For example, if a study examines basic memory processes, can that knowledge about memory be used in an applied setting (such as remembering to take your medication at a specific time)?
5. You can replicate (repeat) a study and add a twist; study the same question but from a different perspective. For example, you could. . .

    . . . use the same variables but operationalize them differently. In the study cited above you might find a different way to operationalize "cognition." Maybe you think that some aspect of attention not considered in the original study would be important to consider. You could redo the study using this different aspect of cognition.

    . . . test the same variables under different conditions or in combination with other variables. For example, if the participants were tested in a laboratory, you could redo the study in each participant's home. Performance might differ in a more familiar environment. Time of day the testing was done might make a difference. How long the participants had been ill might be an important variable to add.

    . . . include original population and another population to see if the finding holds true for both groups. For example, does illness have the same effect on middle age adults as it did in these very old adults? How about comparing older adults who live with others (either family or in an assisted living community) to those who live alone? Does frequent interaction with other people slow down cognitive decline?

Applying What You Have Read

Find and read the article by Verhaeghen et al. cited above. Propose a new study that builds on this one by using one of the methods described above. This is just for practice; the study you carry out may have nothing to do with this topic. If you cannot get a copy of this article, use one you have included in your literature review or another one suggested by your instructor.

In the new study based on Verhaeghen et al. . . .

1. What is the IV? How is it operationalized?

_____

_____

2. What is the DV? How is it operationalized?

_____

_____

3. Describe the research question to be investigated by the new study. What will be the purpose of this new study?

_____

_____

_____

_____

_____

4. Write a hypothesis that applies to this research question. Remember that a good hypothesis is testable. It must make a specific prediction about variables that are clearly operationalized. It must predict some change (in other words, don't propose the null—no change—hypothesis). A good hypothesis should logically follow from findings in the existing literature and be based on theory.

_____

_____

_____

_____

_____

_____

_____

The Structure of <u>Your</u> Study

Now you are going to apply this thought process to the topic you have chosen. Answer the questions below about the study you will design for your own project. Put lots of detail into your answers; this information will serve as the basis of your Method section in your paper.

1. Briefly describe the problem area. Propose a research question.
2. State your hypothesis.

(answer *either* #3 *or* #4, depending on the method you will use in your study)

3. If you are using an *experimental* method or a *nonexperimental* method that compares group means (such as an *ex post facto* study) . . .
   a. State your independent variable(s) and provide an operational definition. Specify the levels of your IV.
   b. State your dependent variable and provide an operational definition. What kind of measurement will you use (i.e., frequencies, correctness, etc.)? What kind of instrument will you use?
4. If you are using a *correlational* design, specify the design and the variables to be used and operationalize the variables.
   Note that your study will be either a comparison of group means or a comparison of rank order (a correlational study)—not both.
5. What extraneous variables exist and how can you control them?
6. Describe your method.
   a. *Participants*. Who will they be, how will you find them? How many will you need? How will you assign them to your groups? Provide a copy of your informed consent form (sample in the lab on correlations—this time you get to copy; replace the italicized portions with your own material).
   b. *Materials*. What will you use to collect the data? Provide copies of your measurement tools. Give lots of details about your materials.
   c. *Design*. What research design will you use? See the following Web sites for help in deciding.

   http://www.socialresearchmethods.net/selstat/ssstart.htm
   http://www.wadsworth.com/psychology_d/templates/student_resources/
       workshops/stat_workshp/chose_stat/chose_stat_01.html

   d. *Procedure*. What exactly (step by step) will happen in the experimental session? Give enough detail that a person who wasn't there could replicate your study.
7. What ethical considerations are there and what will you do about them? Refer to the relevant chapter in your textbook for ideas.
8. Results. What analysis will you use? Use the analysis decision tree below to help you decide. Briefly describe what statistical outcome would support your hypothesis.
9. Go one step further. Many journals prefer to publish "multi-study" articles. These articles report on research that was carried out in a series of studies rather than just one. The first study may have raised an additional issue that was then tested in the second study. Suppose you find the results you anticipate. What additional questions might your study raise about the topic?

Suggest a "Study Two" for your project that follows up on the findings of the first one.

Moving Along

You are now ready to write the first draft of your final paper. See Appendix 1 for specific instructions for both the first draft and final version of your paper.

Sharing What You Know

After you have read the relevant literature, planned your project, collected and analyzed your data, and interpreted it, you need to communicate it to other researchers and interested parties. You may have the most astounding research results ever, but unless you disseminate what you know, it is worthless. Scientists usually communicate in one or more of three ways: writing, speaking, or by poster. This entire lab manual instructs you on how to write about your findings. Information on oral presentations is found in Lab 8, and instructions on creating a poster are in Lab 12.

Closure

Which Analysis Do I Use for My Design?

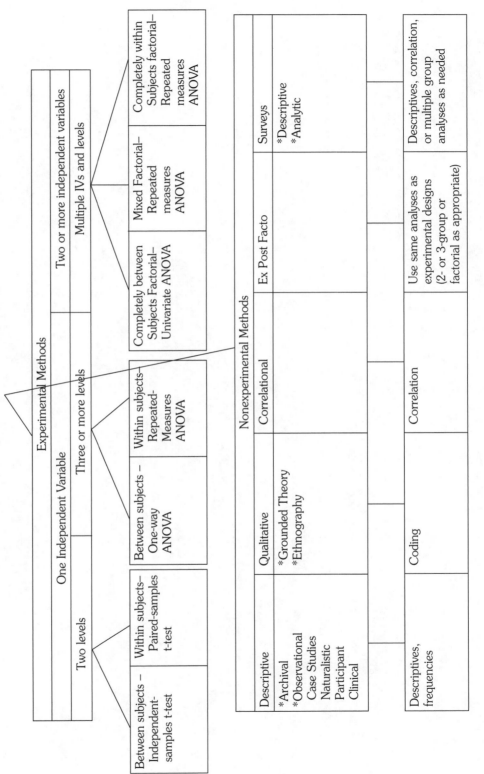

Writing a Discussion Section

Comparative Psychology

DR. W. SCOTT TERRY

Simply put, comparative psychology "compares" species. It has traditionally focused on the comparison of animal species in their psychological functions, such as sensory capacity and learning, and their behaviors, such as reproduction. Contemporary comparative cognition is especially interested in memory, problem-solving and communication capacities of animals in comparison to humans. Comparative psychology adopts behavioral, cognitive, and evolutionary approaches to psychology.

Assignment

In my experience the Discussion section of a paper is the hardest for students to write. This is not surprising, because this is the part of the paper where you go beyond reporting your results and interpret them. Since you don't yet have a lot of background knowledge on your topic and haven't read the associated literature thoroughly, you may come up blank when trying to interpret what you've found. Years of study will provide you with knowledge about your topic; for now we'll just concentrate on what sort of information should go in a Discussion section. Your assignment for today will be to analyze a Discussion section and then write one of your own. Turn in: an original Discussion section for data presented below.

Topic

Studying the visual acuity of sea turtles

Target Article

Bartol, S. M., Mellgren, R. L., & Musick, J. A. (2003). Visual acuity of juvenile loggerhead sea turtles (Caretta caretta): A behavioral approach. *International Journal of Comparative Psychology, 16*(2–3), 143–155.

Have you ever noticed that your vision underwater is different from your vision on land? I am very nearsighted, but can see fairly well underwater. Sea turtles spend most of their time in the water, but come on land to lay eggs. Like me, they are nearsighted on land. These experimenters used operant conditioning (you probably studied this back in Introductory Psychology) to figure out just how well turtles can see in the water. The turtles were rewarded (raw squid—yum!) when they correctly distinguished between two different visual patterns. Once the turtles were trained, the stimuli were made smaller and smaller until the turtles could no longer tell the difference. The smallest size at which they could distinguish the patterns indicated their acuity.

When writing a Discussion section, bear in mind that your reader, although probably educated, may not be an expert in your particular area. You need to use the Discussion section to make clear to that reader what was found and what it means. Don't assume that your readers will be familiar with your topic.

Discussion Section Checklist

_____**Summarize your findings.** Pull out the important information and organize it for your reader.

_____**Did your findings support or not support your hypotheses?** You began with specific predictions, research questions, or purposes. Now tell the reader whether the findings are consistent with your hypotheses.

_____**Help the reader see the connections between your findings and those previously reported in the literature.** Remember all those studies you cited in the introduction? How do your findings fit in with this larger picture? Refer back to those studies already cited and explain how your results are consistent with or contradictory to earlier studies.

_____**So what does it *mean*?** Even though I already know that one group was significantly different than another (or two variables were positively correlated), what does that really mean?

_____**The good, the bad, and the ugly.** Point out explicitly the ways in which your study makes a unique contribution to the literature. Acknowledge the limitations of your study.

_____**Where do we go from here?** So now what? What do your findings suggest for applications or future research? Can you make any recommendations based on your work? For example, in Zimbardo's study cited in an earlier lab, what changes to prison policies might the author have suggested? What factors should be considered by future studies?

Look at the Discussion section of an article you have used in your project (first choice, because you now have some background knowledge about your chosen topic), the article listed above, or another one assigned by your instructor. Work with a partner to find where the author(s) addressed (or failed to address) each of these points. I will illustrate this assignment using the Discussion section from the Bartol et al. (2003) article cited above.

Summarize your findings. Bartol et al. do this in the third paragraph on p. 151, where they report the visual acuity of juvenile loggerhead turtles. The first two paragraphs set the stage for interpreting the finding. Other authors prefer to begin the discussion section by summing up their most important findings. Additional findings are mentioned in the bottom paragraph on p. 152.

Did your findings support or not support your hypotheses? This study was more exploratory than experimental. The authors didn't predict what the acuity would be; rather they simply set out to discover it. Their findings allowed them to draw some conclusions about the turtles' visual acuity.

Help the reader see the connections between your findings and those previously reported in the literature. This was done throughout the Discussion section. For example, the 3rd paragraph refers to studies that have addressed the same issue using other methodologies. Other studies have examined turtles' visual acuity on land rather than in water. On p. 152 and p. 153 the authors refer to work examining the acuity of other aquatic species. Notice how the discussion moves from the specific (other turtle studies) to the more general (other species).

So what does it *mean*? The meaning is fairly straight-forward in this article; the authors demonstrated new information about visual acuity in turtles. However, the authors helped the reader see how the results might complement findings about the structure of turtle brains. Their findings can also be used to understand how turtles use visual information to carry out important turtle stuff, like finding food, avoiding becoming somebody else's food, defending territory, etc. It may also have implications for turtle conservation efforts.

The good, the bad, and the ugly. This is noted in the first two paragraphs of the discussion. What was good about their methodology? What limitation existed? Another strength is mentioned in the last paragraph.

Where do we go from here? The authors noted that a future study might test other visual dimensions, such as brightness.

Now it's your turn. Using the data from one of the labs already completed (for example, the correlation design), discuss with a partner how you could address each of the parts of the discussion listed above for a lab report. Write a short Discussion section on the material, then exchange papers with your partner. Each of you check the contents of what your partner wrote against the checklist above. Your instructor may want you to turn in your Discussion section.

Closure

By now you are experienced at writing an APA style paper. If, when you complete your research project and hand in your final paper, you think your paper turned out to be pretty good, consider submitting it to one of the journals devoted to publishing undergraduate papers. For example, see the following sites:

The Undergraduate Journal of Psychology
  http://www.psych.uncc.edu/journal.htm

Canadian Undergraduate Journal of Cognitive Science
  http://www.sfu.ca/cognitive-science/journal/

Psi Chi Journal
  http://www.psichi.org/pubs/journal/submissions.asp

UCLA Undergraduate Psychology Journal
  http://www.studentgroups.ucla.edu/upj/

Journal of Psychological Inquiry
  http://puffin.creighton.edu/psy/journal/JPIhome.html

URC Undergraduate Research Journal
  http://www.kon.org/CFP/cfp_urjhs.html

Great Plains Students' Psychology Convention
  http://www.psych-central.com/gpconv.htm

The Wide World of Psychology

I do not want to imply that the areas of psychology featured in these labs represent a complete picture of the myriad faces of psychology. There are many fascinating areas that weren't included for lack of space. For example, just among my colleagues the following areas are represented: Human Sexuality, Psychology of Women, Developmental Psychopathology, Biopsychology, Evolutionary Psychology, Sports Psychology and Quantitative Psychology. There's something for almost everyone. Check out the Web sites below to learn about more areas in psychology.

Best wishes as you shape your future career in psychology—or whatever career you eventually decide upon.

http://www.apa.org/about/division.html
http://psych.hanover.edu/gradframe.html
http://www.psywww.com/careers/specialt.htm
http://psychology.about.com/library/weekly/aa021503a.htm
http://psychology.about.com/od/moreareas/
http://www.socialpsychology.org/psylinks.htm

Appendixes

Appendix 1

Instructions for Papers

Instructions for Literature Review

BEFORE you write your literature review, look through all of the pages from the *APA Publication Manual* that are listed under "FAQs about APA Style."

 NEXT, if you have not already done so, read the section on "Writing It" found at http://depts.washington.edu/psywc/handouts.shtml. Scroll down and click on "Bem: Writing the empirical journal article." Read down through the subsection entitled "Criticizing Previous Work." Also read the section entitled "Common Errors of Grammar and Usage."

**Start with an outline. See
http://owl.english.purdue.edu/handouts/general/gl_outlin.html for help
on developing an outline.**

BEFORE you turn your literature review in, **check it** against these instructions to make sure you met all the requirements.

1. Include a title page with header and running head (see *APA Publication Manual*), text, and a reference page.
2. Text should be at least _____ pages long and include at least _____ references. At least _____ references should be **primary source** articles (i.e., report original research—they will have a Method section, Results, etc.) from **peer-reviewed journals**. Check with your instructor if you are unsure if a particular journal is suitable. Do not cite Web sites that aren't peer-reviewed. Limit the number of direct quotes used in your paper. Use a direct quote if it adds value to your paper; otherwise, tell about it in your own words.
3. Your paper should be typed using a size 12 font, double-spaced, and have 1 inch margins all around.

4. Remember, writing counts! Go through at least two drafts of your paper. Ask someone to read it critically and give feedback.

5. Try to avoid the "grocery list syndrome" in which a series of studies are described. Talk about a topic, an issue, or a problem and bring in the references to support what you are saying. Integrate the studies you report.

6. References must be cited in the text and also listed on the reference page using proper APA format. If you cite it in the text, it must also be on the reference page.

7. Attach a copy of your outline to the back of your paper.

Ask for help if you need it. <u>Avoid plagiarism by closing sources before you type</u>.

Instructions for First Draft of The Final Paper

 BEFORE you begin to write, go to the Bem article at http://depts. washington.edu/psywc/handouts.shtml, and read, beginning with "Ending the Introduction" and ending with "The Method Section."

1. Your paper will include:
   a. Title page with header and running title.
   b. Introduction: This is your literature review, incorporating any changes suggested in the earlier draft. At the end, segue from the existing literature into the purpose of your study and include your hypothesis.
   c. Method: The method section will have several subheadings: participants, materials, and design and procedure. Be detailed. The goal of the method section is to make it so explicit that someone who wasn't there can copy your study. Use the future tense in your descriptions because, for most of you, data collection has not yet taken place. What extraneous variables existed and how will you control for them? You don't yet know the details about your participants, but describe how many you will try to recruit, where they will come from, and any other characteristics you expect to find.
   d. Results: In a few sentences, describe how you will analyze your data (what kind of statistical test) and describe the pattern of findings that would support your hypothesis.
   e. Reference page.

2. Before you turn your paper in, check it against the APA section of your text or the related pages in the *APA Publication Manual*.

3. If you have made up your own instrument, include a copy of it in an Appendix.

Instructions for Final Paper

 BEFORE you begin to write, go to the Bem article at http://depts. washington.edu/psywc/handouts.shtml, and read the section entitled

"The Results Section" (read all the subheadings, including the ones about the Discussion section and Title and Abstract).

Your final paper should be a complete report of your research project, written in APA style.

1. Your paper will include the following:
   a. Title page with header and running title.
   b. Abstract: It is best to write the abstract after the rest of the paper is finished. In a few sentences describe your procedures, your major results and whether your hypothesis was supported.
   c. Introduction: This is your literature review, incorporating any changes suggested in the earlier draft. At the end, segue from the existing literature into the purpose of your study and include your hypotheses.
   d. Method: This is what you provided in your first draft, but also include any modifications you may have made as you actually carried out your data collection. Also include any changes I suggested in the earlier draft. Make sure you have switched the verb tenses to past tense this time.
   e. Results: Run the appropriate analyses and report your findings as we've practiced in class. Tell which analyses you did and include all the important details, including relevant means and standard deviations either in the text or in a table. Report all findings that relate to your hypotheses, even those that aren't significant.
   f. Discussion: Were your hypotheses supported? If not, speculate on what you might have done differently to obtain the desired results. What limitations hindered your study? How do your findings relate to the literature you discussed earlier? What are the real-world implications of your findings?
   g. References: Use correct APA style!!! Double check the *APA Publication Manual* for correct format.
   h. Appendix: Include copies of any questionnaires, tests, stories, etc. that you used in your experiment.
   i. Tables and graphs (if needed—there is usually no need to duplicate information in a graph that's already in a table): Tables, graphs, or appendixes must be referred to in your text (i.e., "see Table 1"). Notice in your *APA Publication Manual* the correct order for each element of your paper.
2. Before you turn your paper in, check it against the APA section of your text or the related pages in the *APA Publication Manual*.

Appendix 2

SPSS Instructions

Setting Up the SPSS Data File

Open SPSS. You'll see a box that asks "What would you like to do?" Click *Type in data* and *OK*. Now you have a blank spreadsheet. Let's start by labeling the variables. In the bottom-left corner, click the tab that says *variable view*. Next to the number 1 enter [firstvariablename] then [nextvariablename] next to the number 2 (you don't need the brackets). Just so I'll remember later, I enter a description of each variable under "label." That way I'll know later exactly what I meant by each variable name. It also helps you interpret the output of SPSS as you'll see later. Now click the tab that says *data view*. Type in the data.

In my experience, you can never save your data too often. Save by clicking *File* in the top left corner, then *save as*. Specify the drive and file name you want, then click *Save*. Thereafter you can simply click *Save* or the save icon if you'd like to complete the process more quickly.

Finding Descriptive Statistics

Click *Analyze, Descriptive statistics, Descriptives.* Move the dependent variables into the variable box by highlighting each and clicking the arrow to the right. When they have both been moved, click *OK*.

Paired-Samples t-test

Click *Analyze, Compare means, Paired-samples t-test.* Click both variables to be compared, then the right arrow to move them into the paired variables box. Click *OK*.

Independent-Samples t-test

Click *Analyze, Compare means, Independent-samples t-test.* Move the dependent variable into the "Test Variable" box, and the independent variable into the "Grouping Variable" box. Click *Define groups.* Enter the numbers you used to designate your groups. For example, if your IV was age, you may have designated younger as 1 and older as 2. Click *Continue* and *OK.*

Correlation

Click *Analyze, Correlate,* then *Bivariate.* Highlight the names of the two variables and click the arrow to the right to move them into the variable box. Now click *OK.*

One-way Analysis of Variance (ANOVA)

Click *Analyze, Compare means, One-way anova.* Move the DV score to the "Dependent" box and IV to the "Factor" box. There are a variety of ways you could do post hoc tests should they be needed. For now click *Post hoc, Tukey, Continue.* You'll want to compare the means for the groups, so click *Options, Descriptive, Continue, OK.*

Univariate ANOVA

Click *Analyze, General linear model, Univariate.* Move the IV(s) into the Fixed Factors box and the DV into the Dependent Variable box. Go to *Options,* and click the box to the left of *Descriptives.* Finish with *Continue, OK.*

Repeated Measures ANOVA

Click *Analyze, General linear model, Repeated measures.* Now you are asked for a within-subject factor name. This is the repeated measures IV. Name the within-subject factor something that makes sense, indicate the number of levels, then click *Add, Define.* Highlight the three levels of the IV and move them into the "Within-subjects Variables" box. If you also have a between subject variable (such as would be the case in a mixed factorial design), enter that in the box labeled "Between-Subjects Factor(s)." Click *Options, Descriptive Statistics, Continue, OK.*

Appendix 3

Chi-Square Analysis

Using a *t* test or ANOVA is well and good when comparing group means, but what if you want to compare counts (how many participants were in each cell)? In this case you are using nominal data. Let me give you an example. Let's say you wonder whether children in either kindergarten or 1st grade will pick up a handgun (definitely one that is not loaded—I'd have a police officer on the scene when I collected data, just to be safe) when they find it among toys. Let's say the children had been told to never touch a gun. Who will be most likely to pick up the gun? In this case you just want a count. You can analyze the data using a chi (rhymes with pie)-square (χ^2) analysis. BTW, I got the fancy χ by using the "insert, symbol" feature of the word processing program.

Suppose this is what you find:

Grade: 1 = kindergarten, 2 = 1st grade
Gun: 1 = picked up gun, 2 = did not pick up gun

grade	gun
1.00	1.00
1.00	1.00
1.00	1.00
1.00	1.00
1.00	1.00
1.00	1.00
1.00	1.00
1.00	1.00
1.00	1.00
1.00	1.00
1.00	2.00
1.00	2.00
1.00	2.00
1.00	2.00

grade	gun
1.00	2.00
1.00	2.00
1.00	2.00
1.00	2.00
1.00	2.00
1.00	2.00
2.00	1.00
2.00	1.00
2.00	1.00
2.00	1.00
2.00	1.00
2.00	1.00
2.00	1.00
2.00	1.00
2.00	1.00
2.00	1.00
2.00	1.00
2.00	1.00
2.00	1.00
2.00	1.00
2.00	1.00
2.00	1.00
2.00	2.00
2.00	2.00
2.00	2.00

Enter these data into a data file.

1. Click *Analyze*
2. *Descriptives*
3. *Crosstabs*. Enter one variable in the row box and one in the column box.
4. Click *Statistics*
5. *Chi square*
6. *Continue*
7. *OK*.

Gun * Grade Crosstabulation

	Count		
	Grade		
	kindergarten	1st grade	
picked up gun	10	17	27
did not pick up gun	10	3	13
Total	20	20	40

Just by looking at the table, we can see that kindergarten children are just as likely to pick up the gun as not, whereas 1st graders are much more likely to pick it up. Just because the data appear to support that conclusion is not enough; we have to back it up with some type of statistics.

Chi-Square Tests

	Value	df	Asymp. Sig. (2-sided)	Exact Sig. (2-sided)	Exact Sig. (1-sided)
Pearson Chi-Square	5.584[a]	1	.018		

[a]0 cells (.0%) have expected count less than 5. The minimum expected count is 6.50.

The χ^2 compares the number of children in each cell against what might be expected if neither variable influenced how many children picked up the gun to how many children actually ended up in each cell. In this case the chi square is significant, and has 1 degree of freedom.

You would report the chi square like this:

$\chi^2 (1, N = 40) = 5.58, p = .018$

So . . . we need to amend the table found at the end of the lab on *Designing Your Study* to include the χ^2, which can be used when you are measuring counts instead of means.

Graphing

When the IV Is a Between-Subjects Variable

Use the data from the lab on the Two-Group design, between-subjects.

1. Click *Graphs*
2. *Bar*
3. *Simple*
4. *Summaries for groups of cases*
5. *Define*
6. *Other statistic* (You would select other statistic because we are reporting means instead of counts.) Select the DV and move it to "variable box." Select the IV, move it to "category axis."
7. Finish with *OK*. You can follow the same procedure for a line graph.

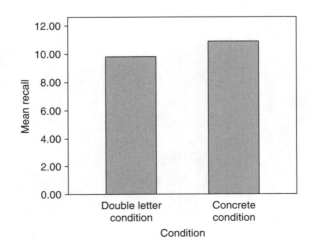

When the IV Is a Within-Subjects Variable

Use the data from the lab on the Two-Group design, within-subjects.

1. Click *Graphs*
2. *Bar*
3. *Simple*
4. *Summaries for separate variables*
5. *Define.* Move the two variables to be compared to the box labeled "bars represent" then
6. Click *OK.* Because the means are the same for both designs, the graphs should look alike.

Effect Size

In this appendix I'm not writing about an area of psychology, but rather about a concept in psychology (and related disciplines). There is a movement within health care to integrate care of both mental and physical health. Traditionally, physical and mental disorders have been treated in isolation from each other, reflecting a tendency to think of mind and body as separable (blame it on Descarte, a 17th century philosopher). More and more, however, we are coming to understand—or at least respect—mind/body interactions. What you think or your mental state might be able to heal or hurt you. Physical illness can have mental consequences. Dr. Ronald Levant, president of the APA at the time of this writing, called for more integration of health care,[1] in which one treats the whole person rather than just the body or the mind. In this scenario, physicians and psychologists would work together to treat patients. Psychological interventions would be used along with traditional (and perhaps nontraditional) health care approaches to treat illness and injury. For example, relaxation techniques have been used to counteract the deleterious effects of stress hormones in conditions such as hypertension, depression, and insomnia.[2]

Note two things in the article cited below. First, notice how writing was used to manage physical pain in women with fibromyalgia. Second, notice how the authors put the significant group differences in perspective by including estimates of effect size.

Is there a distinction between *significant* differences and *meaningful* differences? In other words, is the significance level produced by an analysis a good measure to use to decide if something has "real-world" importance? Is a significance level of .001 necessarily better than a level of .04? In this

---

[1] http://www.apa.org/monitor/may05/pc.html
[2] http://www.apa.org/monitor/may05/physician.html

lab you will learn about the rationale for reporting effect sizes. Turn in: your answers to the questions asked in the body of this lab.

An Example from the Literature

Broderick, J. E., Junghaenel, D. U., & Schwartz, J. E. (2005). Written emotional expression produces health benefits in fibromyalgia patients. *Psychosomatic Medicine, 67*(2), 326–334.

Writing about traumatic experiences has been successfully used in the past to improve health outcomes associated with several disorders such as rheumatoid arthritis, asthma, and breast cancer. The study cited here was intended to determine whether writing could improve psychological and physical well-being among women with fibromyalgia, a disorder associated with chronic pain and fatigue. Ninety-two women were randomly assigned to one of three groups—a "trauma-writing" group, a control writing group, or a group that received standard treatment. Trauma writing refers to an emotional recounting of personal traumatic experience. The control writing group wrote about day-to-day activities. Psychological well-being, pain, and fatigue were assessed at four points in time: prior to receiving treatment, posttreatment, four months later, and 10 months later. Significant reductions in pain (effect size = .49), fatigue (effect size = .62) and improved psychological well-being (effect size = .47) were found at the 4-month follow-up visit, but not at the 10-month follow-up. Trauma writing produced at least short term gains in both psychological and physical outcomes.

For more information on fibromyalgia, see the following Web sites:

http://fmaware.org/fminfo/brochure.htm

http://www.mayoclinic.com/invoke.cfm?id=DS00079

Effect Size

Consideration of effect size is increasingly considered to be important by editors and reviewers. Whether or not you find group differences to be significant is partially driven by sample size. Let's say I want to know if sleep deprivation had an effect on memory ability. Perhaps I had a group of participants memorize something just prior to having a good night's sleep while another group memorized the same material then stayed up all night. If my sample is large enough, even very small differences between the groups would be significant, but how can I tell if the difference is big enough to be meaningful? Sometimes the results of psychological studies are used as the basis of social changes or policies that affect many lives. You wouldn't want to draw a conclusion about, for example, the effects of a particular early intervention program on IQ on the basis of a statistically significant but very tiny group difference. If the early intervention program raised IQ scores by $\frac{1}{2}$ point, is that a big enough improvement to justify spending millions of dollars and years of time on this program? One way to evaluate this is to include a measure of effect size in our analysis. Effect size is an estimate of the magnitude of differences between means in terms of standard deviations or proportions of variance explained.

There are several different measures of effect size, such as the r-Family, and various members of the d-Family. To compare the relative merits of these measures is not our goal here, so we'll talk about partial eta-squared (eta^2) because that is the measure provided by SPSS. The values can range between 0 (meaning that the IV doesn't account for any of the variance in the DV) and 1.00 (meaning that the IV accounts for all of the variance in the DV).

In the target article, effect size was calculated using two methods, a d score as well as a more conservative estimate. The estimates of effect size indicated that not only did "trauma writing" produce a statistically significant change, the change was large, making it more likely that it produced a meaningful change as well. If you were deciding whether to make this part of the standard treatment of fibromyalgia, then you would have a good basis for including it.

Practice Using Effect Size

Let's practice thinking about effect size by using the data you saved from the between subjects Three Groups Design lab. Instead of using the One-Way ANOVA, let's analyze it this time using the general linear model. This will produce the same F score, but it allows us to obtain additional information.

1. Open the saved data file.
2. Click *Analyze*
3. *General linear model*
4. *Univariate*
5. Move the IV into the Fixed Factors box and the DV into the Dependent Variable box.
6. Go to options, and click the box to the left of descriptives
7. and estimates of effect size
8. Finish with *Continue*
9. *OK*

Above is the source table for this analysis. Notice that the F for the IV is 12.925, just like it was when we used One-way ANOVA. This time, however, we also have a value for "partial Eta Squared." In this case, just

Tests of Between-Subjects Effects

			Dependent Variable: Full IQ score			
Source	Type III Sum of Squares	df	Mean Square	F	Sig.	Partial Eta Squared
Corrected Model	1547.267[a]	2	773.633	12.925	.000	.489
Intercept	240665.633	1	240665.633	4020.774	.000	.993
aftr_tbi	1547.267	2	773.633	12.925	.000	.489
Error	1616.100	27	59.856			
Total	243829.000	30				
Corrected Total	3163.367	29				

[a]R Squared = .489 (Adjusted R Squared = .451).

under 50% of the variance in IQ scores can be explained by the amount of time after the injury.

New and Improved Results Section

Rewrite the results section for these data just as you did in the lab on the three-group Design, but this time report the eta^2 values after the significance level (i.e., F, p, eta^2).

_____

_____

_____

_____

_____

_____

If about half of the variance in IQ scores is explained by time after injury (our IV), what is the source of the remaining variance? Obviously other things affect one's IQ score, so one or more other variables, known or unknown, are at work.

How High Is High Enough?

So, is a partial squared eta of .489 high? Low? Midway? This would generally be considered a moderate to high effect size. A somewhat arbitrary but widely used rule of thumb for Cohen's d is that .2 is small, .5 is moderate, and .8 is large. Effect sizes in psychology tend to be low, depending on the nature of the dependent variable. Anything above 0 may be worth talking about, although don't put too much weight on values under .05, whereas a value of .10 may be noteworthy. Look back at the effect sizes reported in the summary of the target article above. Did trauma writing have a big or small effect on the physical and psychological outcome measures?

Estimating Effect Size When Using Other Types of Statistics

You can make estimates of sample size for other types of analyses you've learned about. For example, with a correlation, you can square the r for an estimate of effect size. The lab you did on correlations produced $r = -.685$. Square the r and you have $r^2 = .47$. For correlations, .10 is small, .3 is moderate, and .5 is large. On a t-test, SPSS provides you with confidence intervals for the mean difference between the two variables or groups. The confidence interval tells you the probability that the difference between the two population means falls between two values. For example, let's say your sample means are 102.57 for the control group and 130 for the experimental group. The group means differ from each other by 27.43. If the 95% confidence interval is 23.23 and 31.63, we know that there is a 95% probability that the difference between the population means lies somewhere between 23.23 and 31.63.

To Sum Up . . .

So just because something is statistically significant doesn't necessarily mean it has practical significance. The effect size is a step in deciding how important the difference is, but in the end the effect size has to be interpreted using professional knowledge, judgment, and logic. For example, let's say a study on the ability of Drug X to prevent cancer has an effect size of .10. If that effect size translates into thousands of saved lives, then it may be of practical significance. This is one of those times when your computer can't tell you how to evaluate your data.

Be the Consultant

Let's pretend you are a highly regarded research psychologist in the area of family studies. You have been asked to address a policy-making body on the advisability of implementing an intervention program in which unemployed parents are provided with parenting classes in hopes that this program will raise the school-readiness scores of their preschool children. In general, the research results of studies of this program have produced statistically significant results, showing improved school-readiness scores. For example, one study compared participants who took the parenting classes to those who took classes in gardening and to controls who did not attend any classes. The main effect of condition was significant, $F(2,91) = 4.62$, $p = .001$, $eta^2 = .03$. We'll assume the effect size is representative of most of the studies. What advice would you tell the policy makers about implementing this program on a wide-spread basis? Explain your recommendation.

_____

_____

_____

_____

_____

What would you have advised (and why) had the effect size been .24?

_____

_____

_____

_____

_____

Apply What You've Learned

Now that you've been introduced to the concept of effect size, look for an article that reports effect size. Go to PsycINFO and type in "effect size and _____." Fill in the blank with the topic of your project or any other topic that interests you. For example, my research area is sleep and cognition and behavior in children, so I typed in "effect size and sleep" and found 11 entries. You will need to choose an article from a source available in your library or available full-text on line. Alternatively, your instructor may direct you to or provide you with a specific article to use.*

———————

*One suggestion from a journal likely to be widely available is . . .

Kalman, D., Lee, A., Chan, E., Miller, D. R., Spiro III, A., Ren, X. S., & Kazis, L. E. (2004). Alcohol dependence, other psychiatric disorders, and health-related quality of life: A replication study in a large random sample of enrollees in the Veterans Health Administration. *American Journal of Drug and Alcohol Abuse, 30*(2), 473–486.

Read the article, then briefly describe the purpose and findings of the research, including the effect size.

_____

_____

_____

_____

_____

_____

Which statistic was used to estimate effect size?

_____

What did the effect size tell you about the results?

_____

_____

_____

_____

_____

_____

Closure

To read more about effect sizes see a statistics text book or the following article:

McCartney, K., & Rosenthal, R. (2000). Effect size, practical importance, and social policy for children. *Child Development, 71*(1), 173–180.

You may wish to learn to calculate Cohen's *d* from SPSS output since it is such a widely reported measure of effect size.

$$d = \frac{\text{mean for group 1} - \text{mean for group 2}}{\text{square root of [(squared standard deviation for group 1} + \text{squared standard deviation for group 2)/2]}}$$

Let's say you have found a significant difference between the means of 2 groups having the following values:

	Mean	Standard Deviation
Group 1	10.9	2.36
Group 2	9.8	2.82

$$d = \frac{10.9 - 9.8}{\text{square root of } [2.36^2 + 2.82^2/2]}$$

$$d = \frac{1.1}{\text{square root of } [5.57 + 7.95/2]}$$

$$d = \frac{1.1}{2.6} = .42$$

Calculate the effect size for the following values:

Group Statistics

	group	N	Mean	Std. Deviation	Std. Error Mean
ontask	meds	10	186.0000	32.27658	10.20675
	no meds	10	159.7000	32.02447	10.12703

Practice What You've Learned

The purpose of this section is to give you experience with identifying a design that will test a hypothesis, then specifying how the data should be analyzed. Your instructor may also want you to enter the data and run the appropriate analyses.

Given these variables . . .

Grade in school (early, middle, and late elementary school)
Gender
Socio-economic status (low or middle)
Average hours of sleep
    on school nights (as reported on a sleep diary kept for five school nights)
    on weekend nights
Average "restfulness" of sleep (also indicated on the diary)
Hyperactivity rating (generated using a parent checklist)

. . . and the following data . . .

1.00	1.00	1.00	9.80	9.40	2.70	12.00
1.00	1.00	1.00	10.28	10.00	9.00	13.00
1.00	1.00	1.00	10.20	10.30	3.80	5.00
1.00	1.00	1.00	10.40	10.40	7.50	.00
1.00	1.00	1.00	10.32	10.40	1.90	5.00
1.00	1.00	1.00	10.20	10.12	8.20	2.00
1.00	2.00	1.00	11.00	11.20	9.50	14.00
1.00	2.00	2.00	8.90	8.90	9.93	15.00
1.00	2.00	1.00	9.64	9.50	4.60	7.00
1.00	2.00	2.00	10.10	10.30	5.30	.00
1.00	2.00	1.00	9.00	9.10	3.60	2.00
1.00	2.00	1.00	10.07	10.30	4.80	11.00
1.00	2.00	1.00	9.60	9.50	2.70	6.00
2.00	1.00	2.00	9.78	9.00	3.60	5.00

2.00	1.00	2.00	9.00	8.60	2.20	5.00
2.00	1.00	2.00	10.25	10.00	8.90	3.00
2.00	1.00	1.00	9.50	9.30	3.40	.00
2.00	1.00	2.00	10.18	10.50	6.00	8.00
2.00	1.00	1.00	10.22	10.22	3.60	4.00
2.00	1.00	2.00	9.80	10.00	7.50	3.00
2.00	2.00	1.00	9.33	9.00	4.00	2.00
2.00	2.00	2.00	8.35	9.00	4.40	5.00
2.00	2.00	2.00	10.87	10.50	5.00	7.00
2.00	2.00	2.00	9.32	9.00	4.80	6.00
2.00	2.00	1.00	10.70	10.20	7.20	.00
2.00	2.00	2.00	8.37	9.00	3.80	18.00
3.00	1.00	1.00	8.00	10.00	5.00	2.00
3.00	1.00	2.00	9.46	10.30	5.00	9.00
3.00	1.00	1.00	8.20	10.20	5.00	1.00
3.00	1.00	2.00	7.50	12.00	3.00	6.00
3.00	1.00	1.00	8.83	10.80	3.00	1.00
3.00	1.00	2.00	7.40	11.50	4.00	.00
3.00	2.00	1.00	7.80	12.50	4.60	.00
3.00	2.00	2.00	9.80	10.80	4.80	.00
3.00	2.00	1.00	10.00	11.80	5.60	.00
3.00	2.00	2.00	8.88	9.60	4.20	2.00
3.00	2.00	1.00	7.90	11.00	5.60	2.00
3.00	2.00	2.00	8.00	9.90	5.70	4.00
3.00	2.00	1.00	8.33	11.11	4.20	2.00

. . . see if you can answer the following questions. Identify the design as well as whether it is between subjects, within subjects, or mixed when appropriate.

1. You want to know if boys or girls get more sleep on school nights. To answer this question you would use a _____ design which you would analyze using a(n) _____.
The variables you would include would be (label each as an IV or DV)
_____
_____.
Graph your results.

2. You wonder if hyperactivity decreases with age. To answer this question you would use a _____ design which you would analyze using a(n) _____. The variables you would include would be (label each as an IV or DV) _____
_____.
Assuming your results were significant, would post hoc tests be needed? _____ Which ones might you use? _____
_____

3. You wonder if socio-economic status impacts sleep quality, and whether it is the same for both boys and girls. To answer this question you would use

a _____ design which you would analyze using
a(n) _____. The variables you would include would
be (label each as an IV or DV) _____
_____.

Assuming your results were significant, would post hoc tests be needed?
_____ Which ones might you use? _____

4. Is there a relation between average amount of sleep on school nights and
   hyperactivity level? To answer this question you would use a
   _____ design which you would analyze using
   a(n) _____. The variables you would include
   would be _____
   _____.

   Assuming your results were negative and significant, what can you conclude?
   _____
   _____

   What can you NOT conclude? _____

5. Do boys or girls sleep longer at night, and does it depend on whether it is
   a school night or weekend night? To answer this question you would use a
   _____ design which you would analyze using
   a(n) _____. The variables you would include
   would be (label each as an IV or DV) _____
   _____.

   Assuming your results were significant, would post hoc tests be needed?
   _____ Which ones might you use?
   _____

6. Does socio-economic status vary as a function of grade? In other words,
   are there about the same number of children from low socio-economic status
   homes at each grade level? To answer this question you would analyze it
   using a(n) _____.

Identify some other hypotheses that could be tested using these data.

_____

_____

_____

_____

_____

_____

_____

_____

_____

_____

_____

_____

_____

_____

_____

_____

_____

_____

_____

_____

_____

_____

References in correct APA format – assignment from pp. 26–27

References

Kelly, J. G. (2005). National Institute of Mental Health and the founding of the field of community psychology. In W. E. Pickren, Jr. & S. F. Schneider (Eds.), *Psychology and the National Institute of Mental Health: A historical analysis of science, practice and policy* (pp. 233–259). Washington, DC: American Psychological Association.

Youngstrom, E., Weist, M. D., & Albus, K. E. (2003). Exploring violence exposure, stress, protective factors and behavior problems among inner-city youth. *American Journal of Community Psychology, 32,* 115–129.

(Note that, although the first letters of words in titles are generally lower case, they are capitalized for a proper name – such as National Institute of Mental Health – and in the first word following a colon.)

References

Ahearn, W. H. (2003). Using simultaneous presentation to increase vegetables consumption in a mildly selective child with autism. *Journal of Applied Behavior Analysis, 36*(3), 361–365.

Bartol, S. M., Mellgren, R. L., & Musick, J. A. (2003). Visual acuity of juvenile loggerhead sea turtles (Caretta caretta): A behavioral approach. *International Journal of Comparative Psychology, 16*(2–3), 143–155.

Broderick, J. E., Junghaenel, D. U., & Schwartz, J. E. (2005). Written emotional expression produces health benefits in fibromyalgia patients. *Psychosomatic Medicine, 67*(2), 326–334.

Campbell, C. G., Kuehn, S. M., Richards, P. M., Ventureyra, E., & Hutchinson, J. S. (2004). Medical and cognitive outcome in children with traumatic brain injury. *Canadian Journal of Neurological Science, 31*(2), 213–219.

Cavallo, A., Ris, M. D., & Succop, P. (2003). The night float paradigm to decrease sleep deprivation: Good solution or a new problem? *Ergonomics, 46*(7), 653–663.

Craik, F. I., & Lockhart, R. S. (1972). Levels of processing: A framework for memory research. *Journal of Verbal Learning and Verbal Behavior, 11*(6), 671–684.

Craik, F. I., & Tulving, E. (1975). Depth of processing and the retention of words in episodic memory. *Journal of Experimental Psychology: General, 104*(3), 268–294.

Giacobbi, P. R. Jr., Hausenblas, H. A., Fallon, E. A., & Hall, C. A. (2003). Even more about exercise imagery: A grounded theory of exercise imagery. *Journal of Applied Sport Psychology, 15*(2), 160–175.

Hamrick, H., Cohen, S., & Rodriguez, M. S. (2002). Being popular can be healthy or unhealthy: Stress, social network diversity, and incidence of upper respiratory infection. *Health Psychology, 21*(3), 294–298.

Haney, C., & Zimbardo, P. (1998). The past and present of U.S. prison policy. *American Psychologist, 53*(7), 709–727.

Holt, D. J., Phillips, K. A, Shapiro, E. R., & Becker, A. E. (2003). "My face is my fate": Biological and psychosocial approaches to the treatment of a woman with obsessions and delusions. *Harvard Review of Psychiatry, 11*(3), 142–154.

Kalman, D., Lee, A., Chan, E., Miller, D. R., Spiro III, A., Ren, X. S., & Kazis, L. E. (2004). Alcohol dependence, other psychiatric disorders, and health-related quality of life: A replication study in a large random sample of enrollees in the Veterans Health Administration. *American Journal of Drug and Alcohol Abuse, 30*(2), 473–486.

Kenrick, D. T., Keefe, R. C., Gabrielidis, C., & Cornelius, J. S. (1996). Adolescents' age preferences for dating partners: Support for an evolutionary model of life-history strategies. *Child Development, 67*(4), 1499–1511.

Lang, A. R., Goeckner, D. J., Adesso, V. J., & Marlatt, G. A. (1975). Effects of alcohol on aggression in male social drinkers. *Journal of Abnormal Psychology, 84*(5), 508–518.

Leger, D., Guilleminault, C., Bader, G., Levy, E., & Paillard, M. (2002). Medical and socio-professional impact of insomnia. *Journal of Sleep and Sleep Disorders Research, 25*(6), 621–625.

McCartney, K., & Rosenthal, R. (2000). Effect size, practical importance, and social policy for children. *Child Development, 71*(1), 173–180.

Nalwa, K. & Anand, A. P. (2003). Internet addiction in students: A cause of concern. *CyberPsychology and Behavior, 6*(6), 653–656.

Nathanson, R., & Saywitz, K. J. (2003). The effects of the courtroom context on children's memory and anxiety. *Journal of Psychiatry and Law, 31*(1), 67–98.

Renner, M. J., & Scott, M. R. (1998). A life stress instrument of classroom use. *Teaching of Psychology, 25*(1), 46–48.

Verhaeghen, P., Borchelt, M., & Smith, J. (2003). Relation between cardiovascular and metabolic disease and cognition in very old age: Cross-sectional and longitudinal findings from the Berlin Aging Study. *Health Psychology, 22*(6), 559–569.

Zugazaga, C. (2004). Stressful life event experiences of homeless adults: A comparison of single men, single women, and women with children. *Journal of Community Psychology, 32*(6), 643–654.

Index